PLAY MORE BRIDGE

By
Mary A. McVey

Edited by
Linda Roberts Lehtomaa

A Publication of KET
600 Cooper Drive
Lexington, KY 40502
(606) 233-3000
(800) 354-9067

I have written this book with love for Waddill, John, Sally, Kathy, Frank, and Caroline, in hopes that someday they will love bridge as much as their grandmother does.

M.A. McV.

ISBN 0-910475-32-6

KET
600 Cooper Drive
Lexington, KY 40502
(606) 233-3000
(800) 354-9067

I would especially like to thank the American Contract Bridge League (ACBL) for all the help and support throughout the PLAY MORE BRIDGE project.

M. A. McV.

TABLE OF CONTENTS

PREFACE

From the rank beginner who has just started to play bridge, to those of us who have spent countless hours for countless years enjoying it, the wish to PLAY MORE BRIDGE is universal! It's a game for all ages—the very young love it, and, unlike the games of tennis or football or baseball, there never comes a time that we are physically slowed down in our ability to play.

Every time four people sit down for a pleasant session at the bridge table, mistakes will be made and costly lessons will be learned. Some of these lessons will be remembered; others, unfortunately, will be forgotten in time and most probably the mistakes will be repeated. Heavens, we're human, aren't we?

If you spend twenty-four hours a day for the rest of your life playing bridge, there isn't even a remote chance that the same hands would be dealt twice. This is just one of many reasons that the game has fascinated millions of people worldwide for so long.

There are very few statements you can make about bridge that are absolutely 100 percent true all the time, but I can think of three very positive statements that are in that category. First: Nobody is perfect! Second: There is *not* a game in every hand! Third: It's FUN!

We shall talk about lots of hands together and explore many ways of bidding them. In the process, let's hope that we'll all be inspired to PLAY MORE BRIDGE!

INTRODUCTION

Can you, as a bridge lover, think of anything more exciting than having the opportunity to learn more about this game from some of the world's truly great experts? I can't!

How lucky can we be to have this almost unheard-of chance to pick the brains and sit at the feet of such a world famous group as the one that participated in our PLAY MORE BRIDGE show! Champions all!

This little book covers the topics discussed on the television show, with the input from our distinguished guests. All of the sample hands used on the show are included, and many additional ones as well. Each chapter is headed by a few words of wisdom from the expert we heard on the subject on television.

There is so much to be said about our famous giants of bridge and their accomplishments are so unbelievably numerous that a whole book would be needed to list them; so the following is just a very brief word about each one to introduce them to you:

Peter Pender of California has won many titles in bridge competition and is known throughout the world as one of America's leading players. Some of his triumphs have been the Pan-American Invitational Pairs, the Reisinger, the Life Master Men's Pairs, the Grand National Teams, and many others. Besides his skill at bridge, he has many other talents. He is an accomplished pianist, and has won gold medals from both the United States and Canadian Figure Skating Associations. He is a former figure skating coach, and is now the owner and executive director of a California resort.

William S. Root of Boca Raton, Florida, and New York City is outstanding in the world of bridge as a teacher, lecturer, writer, and player! He has won many titles in competition and has represented the United States in world events. He has organized many bridge clubs in the East. He has taught tens of thousands of people the game of bridge and has written several books. Each year he takes a bridge cruise, and hundreds of his followers sign up for the cruise no matter where the ship happens to be going, just for the opportunity of learning more from this great teacher.

Carol Sanders (Mrs. Thomas K.) of Nashville, Tennessee, is one of the outstanding woman players in the world. She has won the World's Women's Pairs and the Venice Trophy (twice), has represented the United States in Mixed Pairs and Mixed Teams competition, and was on the U.S. team that won the Women's World Championship in Seattle at the 1984 Olympiad. Besides these and many other accomplishments, she is the mother of six children and the grandmother of six, and she and her husband are one of the famous couples in the world of bridge.

Thomas K. Sanders of Nashville, Tennessee, is a businessman and developer. He is an outstanding American player and has represented this country many times in world competition. Among his wins are the Spingold, the Blue Ribbon Pairs, and the Life Master Pairs. And he is the only graduate of Vanderbilt University to win the Vanderbilt Trophy. He is a member of the American Contract Bridge League Board of Directors, and is the president-elect of that organization, taking office in January 1986.

Alfred Sheinwold of Los Angeles, formerly of New York City, is a household name to anyone who plays bridge, and even those who have never played bridge have heard of him! He is the author of many very fine bridge books, one of which has sold more than 1,000,000 copies! He has written a series of *Pocket Books of Bridge Quizzes;* he was editor of *The Bridge World* for many years; he was editor of the ACBL *Bulletin;* and he now has a syndicated bridge column. He has won numerous events in competition—and is the captain of the team representing the United States in the World Championship in 1985. A man of many and varied talents, he was the chief code and cipher expert of the OSS during World War II and was also an OSS safecracker! Yet another talent: He sang with the Cantata Singers for ten years! Besides bridge, he's a world-famous authority on backgammon.

Mary Platt Vencill of Berkeley, California, learned to play bridge as a very small child and grew up loving the game. As an adult she became intrigued with duplicate, and is now a tournament director for the American Contract Bridge League. Her special skill is making new players feel at home and happy

13

as they venture into the world of duplicate bridge. This is one reason I especially wanted her on the show. A graduate of Stanford University, Mary is a research analyst, the wife of an economics professor, mother of two children, and—she also happens to be my daughter!

Robert S. Wolff, a Dallas business consultant, is one of the world's greatest players! The list of his many triumphs is staggering! Just to mention a few of them, he has won the Bermuda Bowl three times (that's the trophy for the World Team Championship), the World Open Pairs, the World Mixed Teams, the Pan-American Invitational, the Spingold (three times), the Vanderbilt (three times), and many, many more too numerous to list. He is a star not only as a player but as a writer. His syndicated bridge column, "The Aces," is widely read and very popular.

1
LET'S SUIT OURSELVES

"There are only two basic objectives in bidding: What suit should we name, and how many tricks should we contract? Two full rounds of bidding usually determine what suit, but we often need one more round for how many."

Bobby Wolff

Usually the action at the bridge table is started by a player making a bid of one in a suit. The minute a player opens the bidding, his partner is a happy soul! Whether his hand is good, bad, or indifferent, he is eager to help the opener find the best possible place to play the 26 cards in the combined hands.

Each partner will have decisions to make. These decisions become more difficult when the opponents get into the act—as they most assuredly will if they possibly can. The opening bidder must look to the future before he ever makes a bid and decide how best to cope with all possible responses from his partner. The partner must decide on the best way to describe his hand to the opener.

Any time you have as many as 13 points in your hand, you certainly want to open the bidding—with as many as 14 points, it's an absolute *must!* The partner of the opener, even with as few as six points, should find some way to respond so that the opener will have a chance to bid again.

I'm sure you know the point count for evaluating your hand, but just for the record, here it is. And don't ever forget that your distributional count is as important as high-card count.

High-Card Points	Distributional Points
Ace = 4 points	Doubleton = 1 point
King = 3 points	Singleton = 2 points
Queen = 2 points	Void = 3 points
Jack = 1 point	

So, with all this in mind, let's look at some hands and see how we can best "suit ourselves."

♠ A Q 9 4
♥ A K J 3
♦ 7 5
♣ 8 6 5

This is the sort of hand you're not really wild about, though, of course, you're thankful for those 14 high-card points any way you get them. But this is a tough hand, and one that even the experts don't agree on. Some people never — repeat *NEVER* — bid a major suit without five cards in the suit. I, too, much prefer to hold five. If you are a stickler for this, you'd have to open this hand one club. Personally, with all of the strength in the two four-card major suits, I would open one spade so that I'd have an easy rebid in hearts. I was delighted to

16

find that our distinguished
expert, Mr. Wolff, agreed.

Here is the partner's hand:

♠ 10 3
♥ 8 7
♦ Q J 10 3
♣ K 9 7 4 2

This poor little hand will respond one no trump, and
now the opener will simply
pass. It's as good a contract
as could be hoped for.

This next hand poses no problem. Isn't it a joy
when they're easy!

♠ 5 2
♥ 8
♦ A 8 7 4 2
♣ A K J 10 8

I'm sure all of you know that
when you have two five-card
suits, you always bid the
higher ranking one first. You
must *always* plan ahead and
know what you will do next
time, no matter what partner may respond. So you
open this hand one diamond.
Surely nobody will be lured
into making the wrong bid
just because the club suit is
so much stronger!

Here is partner's hand:

♠ 10 9 6
♥ Q J 9 7 4
♦ K 3
♣ 7 5 2

This hand will respond one
heart, and when opener bids
two clubs, he will pass. For
goodness' sake, don't make
the mistake of bidding
hearts again just because you

17

have five of them! Your hand is very weak, so don't mislead your partner. Besides, if he could have supported your major suit, he most certainly would have. Incidentally, I feel sure that those opponents will be bidding, and they will probably end up playing a spade contract.

Here's a hand with two four-card suits:

♠ K 4
♥ A K 10 3
♦ J 10 2
♣ Q J 9 4

Of course, when you hold two four-card suits that do not touch in rank, you bid the lower ranking suit first—one club. This, too, is planning for the future. In case partner responds with one diamond, you can then bid your hearts at the one level, which is certainly what you want to do with this minimum hand.

Here is partner's hand:

♠ Q 10 9 6 2
♥ J 8 6
♦ 7 5
♣ K 8 7

Partner responds one spade. You are too weak to bid two hearts over the spade response, so you will now bid one no trump, which tells your partner loud and clear that you're minimum.

Now, here's a hand that is very different:

♠ 2	This is a beautiful 19-point
♥ A K 10 7	hand (high cards and distri-
♦ K Q J 9 6 2	bution) and it opens the bid-
♣ K 6	ding one diamond.

Partner has a terrible little hand:

♠ J 9 6 3	In fact, it's so bad that Mr.
♥ Q 8 2	Wolff recommends a pass—
♦ 4 3	and I'm sure he's right. How-
♣ Q 7 5 2	ever, being a cockeyed op-
	timist, I shall respond one
	spade.

Now my partner, with his great big hand, bids two hearts. Heavens, I wish to goodness I had passed because I recognize a *REVERSE* when I hear one. That means I must bid again. So, unhappy as I am, I will have to bid two no trump. A reverse is when a player's second suit ranks higher than his first one, so the bidding is forced to a higher level. The first suit is always longer than the second one, and the hand must be strong (a *minimum* of 16 or 17 points). So, as the weak partner, I'm sorry I didn't take Mr. Wolff's advice and pass the one diamond. But perhaps my partner will bid three diamonds, which he can make.

Here's another interesting hand to make a point:

♠ 9 2	This hand will open the bid-
♥ A K 10 7 5	ding with one heart.
♦ K J 5	
♣ A 6 3	

19

Here is partner's hand:

♠ Q 10 7 3
♥ Q 9 6
♦ Q 6 4 2
♣ 10 9

This is a minimum little hand but certainly worth a response. There is a decision to be made here—whether to bid one spade or raise to two hearts. Well, I've got news for you—that's no decision at all! When your hand is strong enough for one bid only, you should *always* prefer to raise your partner's major suit instead of bidding the other major. On the other hand, if your partner bids a minor suit, you should *always* prefer to bid a four-card major rather than raise a minor. So this hand would bid two hearts.

Here's a hand with two four-card suits:

♠ K J 10 6
♥ A Q 5
♦ 7 3
♣ A Q J 4

Lots of players would open this hand one club and plan to bid the spade suit later. With the combination of these particular hands, it might have been better, but I much prefer to open this hand one no trump.

20

Let's see partner's terrible hand:

♠ Q 9 7 3   It's bad, but the wise course
♥ 10 4   is a pass. If you had had a
♦ K 10 6 5 2   singleton, you would have
♣ 3 2   bid—but more about that
               when we talk about no
               trump bidding. If opener had
               chosen to open the bidding
               one club, the response would
               have been one spade. Opener
               bids two spades and there it
               rests.

Here are two beautiful hands:

♠ A K Q 7 5   This lovely hand will open
♥ K 2   the bidding one spade.
♦ K Q J 3
♣ K 10

Here is partner's hand:

♠ 10 6 4   This hand will raise to two
♥ 8   spades. He has three of his
♦ A 6 5 4 2   partner's suit and a very
♣ Q J 7 3   helpful singleton, but he is
               not strong enough to men-
               tion a new suit at the two
               level. The opener with
               his 21 high-card points will
               immediately bid four
               spades—a very happy con-
               tract.

21

Here's another example:

♠ 7
♥ A Q 10 9 8 5
♦ K Q 10 7
♣ 3 2

This one opens one heart, and when partner makes a jump shift bid of two spades, he will bid three hearts. Partner rebids three spades, and they're both sorry they can't help each other. But they're still magnificent.

Partner's hand:

♠ A K Q 10 8 6
♥ 4 2
♦ A 9 2
♣ A 7

The opener then bids four diamonds. Partner does have two hearts in his hand, so he bids four hearts. This is decision time for the opener. Shall he pass or bid six hearts? Maybe he'll bid six; and if so, he'll have a good shot at it. The opponents will undoubtedly lead a club. Partner will take it with the ace and quickly pitch the losing club on the ace or king of spades.

Here are two hands that present a problem. This situation comes up rather frequently—a misfit.

♠ 7
♥ A Q 10 9 6
♦ K Q J 7 3
♣ Q 4

This hand opens with one heart.

22

This is partner's hand (the opponents do not enter the bidding):

♠ K Q J 8 5 2
♥ 7 3
♦ 2
♣ K 10 5 3

This hand responds one spade—and now the opener bids two diamonds. Now, what shall this hand do? Should he rebid three spades, showing he has a good hand and hopes for game? Or, shouldn't he be able to tell that the hands don't fit and bid only two spades? The correct bid is two spades. If his partner's second suit had been clubs instead of diamonds, it would have been different. No longer a misfit, he would have bid his three spades. That makes sense, doesn't it?

Now we have two hands that shouldn't give anyone trouble:

♠ K Q 7
♥ K 9 3
♦ A K 10 8 4
♣ A 10

This nice hand has 19 high-card points—too much for one no trump and not enough for two no trump. He opens the bidding with one diamond.

This is partner's hand:

♠ 8 5 2   The response from this hand
♥ A J 10 5   is, of course, one heart (re-
♦ Q 6 5 2   member we never raise a
♣ 9 8   minor suit if we have a four-
                 card major). The opening
                 hand now jumps to two no
                 trump, and the partner will
                 bid three no trump. Easy!

Here's another hand where we start with suit bidding but end up playing at no trump, which often
happens:

♠ Q J 10 2   This hand opens the bidding
♥ A Q   with one club.
♦ 10 7
♣ A K 8 5 3

Here is partner's hand:

♠ K 9 6   One diamond is an easy re-
♥ J 5 3   sponse from this hand. The
♦ Q J 8 4 2   opener now bids one spade,
♣ Q 10   and this hand with no trump
                 distribution bids one no
                 trump. Opener has 16 high-
                 card points and decides to
                 bid two no trump. Partner
                 hears the invitation and,
                 hoping to help in his part-
                 ner's clubs and spades, bids
                 three no trump.

Let's take a look at these two hands and make our decision:

♠ A 7 4 3
♥ K Q 10 8
♦ 6 5
♣ A 4 2

This hand has two four-card majors, but look at those spades! The spade suit is very weak. So this is one time he should open the bidding one club. Please remember that the convenient minor suit is only that, a convenience, and should be used only when necessary. Some players can hardly wait to bid a three-card minor on any pretext, which is pretty silly. Anyway, this hand opens one club.

This is partner's hand:

♠ K Q J 8
♥ A 7 3 2
♦ 8
♣ 7 6 5 3

This hand responds one heart, and the opener raises to two hearts. There is no reason to bid the spade suit now when there is such a good fit in hearts, and the opener has a minimum hand which the two-heart bid describes perfectly. The responder has excellent values after hearing the raise, so he decides to bid four hearts. He will lose two clubs and one diamond and make his bid (trumping the fourth club).

25

Here's an interesting hand to think about:

♠ K 6   This very nice hand will
♥ A K J 9 8 4   open one heart.
♦ Q 10
♣ A 3 2

This is partner's hand:

♠ 10 9 7 5   This little six-point hand
♥ 6 2   will respond one spade
♦ A J 4   (please be sure to respond
♣ J 9 5 4   with a four-card major rather
than one no trump). The
opening bidder now jumps to
three hearts, which is a very
strong invitation for partner
to *please* bid if possible.
However, the responder
must decline the invitation
and pass—as he has told his
all in his one bid.

We'll wind up with an interesting, but frustrating,
hand:

♠ A 4 2   This hand opens the bidding
♥ K Q 4   with one diamond.
♦ A 10 9 8 6
♣ 7 5

This is partner's hand:

♠ K Q 7 6
♥ A J 10 2
♦ VOID
♣ K Q J 8 2

This beauty of a hand bids two clubs. He has three biddable suits, so he bids the longest one first. The opener rebids two diamonds, showing his minimum hand. Responder now bids two hearts, which, by changing the suit again, forces another bid from opener. The opener knows his partner has only a four-card heart suit, so he bids two no trump. By this time, responder decides that the hands don't fit well enough to try to bid more, so he just settles for bidding three no trump. And that's the best place to be. There's never a dull moment, is there?

Test Yourself

You are the dealer and hold the following hands. What do you do first? What will you plan to do next?

1. ♠ Q 4 3
   ♥ K J 8 4
   ♦ A 10 9 6
   ♣ K 7

Open one diamond. If partner has a four-card heart suit, he'll bid it and you can raise him. Over any other bid, you will bid no trump (even two clubs, though you don't much like your spade stopper).

2. ♠ A J 9 4 3
   ♥ 6 2
   ♦ K Q 7 4 2
   ♣ 8

Open one spade. This follows the rule of bidding the higher ranking five-card suit first. The only troublesome response would\ be two hearts, which keeps you from bidding your diamonds (because you are too weak). If partner bids two hearts, you have to bid two spades.

3. ♠ A J 9 4 3
   ♥ Q 6
   ♦ K 9 7 4 2
   ♣ 8

This hand looks like the last one, but this queen isn't worth as much as the one in the last hand. You must pass; but, if partner opens, you will want to jump to show a good hand.

4. ♠ 4
   ♥ K 10 9 6
   ♦ A 3
   ♣ A Q 10 6 4 3

No problem opening one club on this hand. If partner bids one diamond, you will, of course, bid one heart. If partner bids one heart, your distribution controls, and those two aces and tens make this hand barely good enough for a jump raise to three hearts. If partner bids one spade or one no trump, you simply bid two clubs. You are not strong enough to reverse.

Now your partner has opened one diamond. What do you do first? What do you plan to do next?

5. ♠ 7 3
   ♥ Q 10 6 4
   ♦ 7 2
   ♣ K Q 9 6 3

Bid one heart. You aren't strong enough to go to the two level. If partner bids one spade, you are still weak, but bid one no trump. If partner bids one no trump, you can bid two clubs, which is *not* forcing (since partner has described his hand as minimum by bidding one no trump).

6. ♠ 7 3
   ♥ A J 10 2
   ♦ 7
   ♣ K Q 9 6 3 2

Now you bid two clubs, intending to bid hearts later (that would be a *reverse* and shows *good* clubs and more than 10 points).

7. ♠ K J 7 4
   ♥ Q 6 3 2
   ♦ 10 9 4
   ♣ 6 3

Bid one heart (the cheapest response). Partner will bid one spade if he has a four-card spade suit, and you will pass as there's no hope for game. You will also pass a one no trump or two diamond bid by opener (both bids deny a four-card spade suit). If partner bids two

29

clubs, you must show your "preference" and bid two diamonds.

8. ♠ A J 8 6 4   Bid one spade, intending to
   ♥ K 10 6 3   bid hearts later. Your partner
   ♦ J 6 3   will then know that you
   ♣ 2   have five spades (see hand
                    above).

9. ♠ Q J 9 7 3 2   Bid one spade, intending to
   ♥ 4   rebid two spades—a sign-off.
   ♦ 8 6   Only if opener's second bid
   ♣ 9 8 7 4   is two clubs would you pass
                    —thankful to have found a
                    fit.

2
VARIOUS NO TRUMPS

"Bidding, just like a language, is the way of communicating with your partner. Whenever you can make a clear, concise statement, your partner always seems to get the message best. Since opening the bidding with some level of no trump sends the message that your hand is balanced (no void, no singleton, and not more than one doubleton) and contains a narrow range of point count, it's to your advantage to open at no trump whenever you can. In other words, your partner will know about what you hold from the first bid—a big advantage!

"It is important for you and your partner to agree on how you proceed after the opening no trump bid. The Stayman Convention is a must! Not using it would be tantamount to sending boys to war without weapons. I also advocate the use of the Jacoby Transfer bids. You'll have fun working these out, and you'll get a lot of satisfaction when you find you are more often getting to the right contract."

Carol Sanders

No trump bidding is a very important part of this game of bridge. You're always pretty happy if you can play a hand at no trump because you only have to make three no trump to score a game, and it's usually easier to take nine tricks than ten or eleven.

I'm sure you know the Standard American System which most players use, but let's go over it quickly just for the record.

Holding	Bid
16–18 high-card points	1 no trump
22–24 high-card points	2 no trump
25–26 high-card points	3 no trump

Your distribution must be 4-3-3-3, 4-4-3-2, or 5-3-3-2. To open one no trump, three suits must be stopped. To open two no trump or three no trump, you should be strong in all four suits. To raise a one no trump bid, partner must have no trump distribution, too. With eight or nine points (or seven with a five-card suit), raise partner to two no trump. With ten points (or nine with a five-card suit), raise partner to three no trump. If your partner opens two no trump, you raise to three with four points.

Let's look at a hand:

♠ A Q 9
♥ K Q 6 2
♦ 7 3
♣ A Q 10 3

This hand has 17 points and no trump distribution, so don't worry about the little worthless diamond doubleton. You can't have everything! With no trump count and distribution, you should certainly bid one no trump.

Most of you are familiar with the Stayman Convention. It's the best thing invented since the wheel! I don't see how we ever managed before Mr. Stayman came up with his great brainchild! Here it is: In response to partner's opening one no trump bid you bid two clubs if your hand contains four-card major suits to see if perhaps the combined hands would play better at a major suit than at no trump. Your two club bid merely asks your partner if he has four cards in a major suit. If he does have, he bids it. If not, he responds two diamonds.

Let's use the previous hand for the opening bidder.

Here is partner's hand:

♠ K J 8 3 2	This hand bids two clubs
♥ J 10 7	over the one no trump open-
♦ Q 2	ing bid. Opener bids two
♣ K 5 2	hearts. This hand now bids
	two spades (promising a five-
	card suit), and they make an
	easy four-spade contract in-
	stead of losing five diamond
	tricks at no trump.

Here's another example:

♠ 4	When partner opens one no
♥ K Q 7 3	trump, even though you
♦ K 7 6 5 3	don't have both major suits,
♣ K 8 6	how could you fail to look
	for a heart fit with this hand?
	So bid two clubs.

Let's take a look at the no trump hand:

♠ K Q 7 6
♥ J 10 9 2
♦ A 8
♣ A Q 4

After his partner bids the Stayman two clubs, this hand bids two spades (when the no trump opener has both four-card majors, he usually bids the spades first). The responding hand is sorry about that, but he has 11 high-card points; and since he knows opener has the spade suit, he bids three no trump. After that bid, the opener stops to think a minute and realizes that his partner would never have used the Stayman bid if he didn't have hearts. So, with four hearts in his hand, he now bids four hearts—which is a splendid contract!

Here's a lulu of a hand that can happen to any of us! Partner opens one no trump. Look at these pitiful 13 cards:

♠ Q 7 6 4
♥ Q 9 4 3
♦ 10 6 5 4 2
♣ VOID

What in the world can you do to save your no trump partner from a hideous fate? Thank goodness for Stayman! You will bid two clubs and, of course, pass *any* response your partner makes. Obviously, he will be very grateful to you whether he

plays the hand at two diamonds, two hearts, or two
spades!

Much as we all love five-card major suits, there
are times when we choose to ignore them when we
bid.

Let's look at one of these times:

♠ A Q	My five-card heart suit is
♥ Q 8 6 3 2	very weak. This hand has 16
♦ Q J 10	points in high cards and also
♣ K Q 4	has no trump distribution,

so I feel that one no trump
is the best description I can
give my partner of this hand.
If he bids two clubs after my
one no trump open, of course
I'll bid my hearts. But if he
doesn't, the hand should
play very well indeed at no
trump.

When the partner of the no trump opening bidder
responds by bidding two diamonds, two hearts, or
two spades, he is waving a red flag! Many people call
this a "drop dead" bid, but I prefer to call it a "rescue!" It says loud and clear, "Partner, my hand is *so*
bad that you can never make your one no trump, but
with your good hand we might have a chance of
making this bid. Anyway, we're better off trying, so
please pass!"

Here is the hand:

♠ 7 6
♥ J 9 8 4 3 2
♦ 10
♣ J 8 3 2

The no trump opener will, of course, pass this hand's two heart bid and be very grateful to him for the rescue from a terrible no trump contract. You will notice that you rescue your partner only when your distribution is unsuitable for no trump. If you had those same cards and normal distribution, you would simply pass.

Suppose the hand looked like this:

♠ 7 6 3
♥ Q J 9
♦ 10 8 4
♣ J 8 3 2

You would pass a one no trump open, as no trump would be as good as, or better than, anything else.

When your partner opens the bidding with one no trump and you have a beautiful suit and a *good* hand, you must be sure to tell your partner by jumping in your suit! You know the combined hands will play better there than at no trump and you may even envision a slam!

36

Here's an example:

♠ 4
♥ A K 10 8 7 6
♦ K 3
♣ Q J 7 5

What a beauty! You will bid three hearts over your partner's opening no trump, and then you and your partner will decide how many to bid for the final contract.

There is a very interesting and valuable convention that I'd like to recommend to you. It was dreamed up by Oswald Jacoby, who was one of the all-time greats in the world of bridge. It is called the Jacoby Transfer. If you and your partner decide to use the Jacoby Transfer, you'll be happy to see that it does not interfere with the use of the Stayman Convention—or with the normal raises at no trump. Its purpose is to do away with the trauma of having the good no trump hand exposed as the dummy after a "rescue" bid. When the opponents can see all those high cards on the board, it is a tremendous advantage for them. So, if you have one of those terrible hands and want to save your partner from playing a miserable no trump by bidding your heart suit, you would bid the suit *under* the heart suit which, of course, is diamonds. That asks the no trump opener to please bid the suit which ranks just above that bid. In this way, the strong no trump hand is declarer and the bad hand is the dummy!

Let's look at two hands and see how it works:

Here is your hand:

♠ A 7 5
♥ A Q
♦ K 9 8 3 2
♣ K Q 10

And here is partner's:

♠ J 10 9 8 6 4
♥ 2
♦ Q 7 5 4
♣ 6 2

You open the bidding one no trump. Partner bids two hearts, and, as you are playing Jacoby, you obediently transfer by bidding two spades and your partner passes. The weak hand is the dummy and it is an excellent contract.

To simplify all this and organize our thinking, here is a little chart that shows what partner's bid means with Stayman and Jacoby. I open one no trump, and:

Partner Bids:	He Asks Me To:
Two clubs	(Stayman) Please bid your four-card major.
Two diamonds	Please bid two hearts.
Two hearts	Please bid two spades.
Two spades	Please bid three clubs.
Two no trump	Please pass with minimum; bid three no trump with maximum.
Three clubs	Please bid three diamonds.

38

Here is another way the Jacoby Transfer bid may be used to an advantage. Let's look at two other hands:

Here is your hand:

♠ J 8
♥ K Q 3
♦ A Q 7 4
♣ K J 4 2

This is partner's hand:

♠ 7 5 3
♥ J 10 8 7 6
♦ K J 2
♣ A Q

You open one no trump and partner bids two diamonds, so you dutifully bid two hearts. Now your partner, who has 11 high-card points, bids three no trump to tell you he has that strength and to leave the decision of the final contract to you. You look at your hand, and because of the weak spade doubleton, decide that four hearts is your bid. Very smart because you could not have made three no trump, and four hearts is easy!

You use both Stayman and the Jacoby Transfer over two no trump opening bids, too. Don't forget that the point count for two no trump is 22-24.

Here are two good examples—both hopeless hands until partner opens two no trump:

♠ J 9 7 6
♥ A 4 3 2
♦ 10 9
♣ 8 6 5

This hand would bid Stayman (three clubs) to check on major suits. You would *never* pass because it takes only four points to raise partner. So if partner does not have a four-card major, you bid three no trump. If he does have one, you bid four of his major suit.

♠ J 8 7 3 2
♥ 10 7
♦ A 8 7
♣ 5 4 3

Your partner opens two no trump and you are delighted to bid three hearts (transfer to three spades) and follow that up with three no trump to give your partner a choice of contracts.

Here is the opener's hand:

♠ A K 10
♥ A 9
♦ K Q 9 6
♣ K Q J 2

After your three no trump bid, this hand decides that four spades will be a better contract. And, oh how wise he is! Look at the weakness in the heart suit!

Before we leave this subject, let me say that it is perfectly all right to use Stayman and Jacoby Transfer bids over a three no trump opener, too. However, you'd use Stayman on hands when you hope to bid a slam if you find out the right information.

Transfers over three no trump opening bids should be used on hands like this:

♠	3	You will bid four diamonds
♥	J 10 6 4 3 2	to make your partner trans-
♦	9 7 4 2	fer to four hearts—which
♣	8 7	you will quickly and happily
		pass.

I'm sure you will all remember that when partner opens at no trump and you bid four no trump, it is *not* Blackwood—but it is a no trump raise which asks your partner to bid six no trump if his bid is maximum and to pass if it is minimum. If he opens one no trump and you have 15 points, you bid four no trump because your 15 plus the maximum 18 equals 33 points—enough for slam. If you have nine points when your partner opens two no trump, you will bid four no trump. If you have as many as 11, you just bid six. It's all a matter of simple arithmetic—your count plus your partner's.

There is another type of no trump that some players choose to bid. It is called the "weak no trump" and is made on hands with no trump distribution and 12-14 high-card points. The partner must have 12 points to raise to two no trump or 14 points to raise to three no trump. If you and your partner decide to play the weak no trump, you must, of course, inform your opponents about your system.

41

Here is a sample hand:

♠ K J 6
♥ Q J 10 5
♦ A 7 3
♣ Q 4 2

I personally do not use this bid, though players who do like it seem to think it has merit. However, I think most players agree that you can't go wrong if you stick to the Standard American System.

Test Yourself

Playing the Standard American System, your partner opens the bidding one no trump. What is your call?

1. ♠ K J 3
   ♥ Q 5 3
   ♦ K J 6
   ♣ 9 8 7 5

   Bid three no trump. You have the right distribution and 10 points.

2. ♠ 10 9 8 6 5 4
   ♥ 6 3
   ♦ J
   ♣ 8 6 4 2

   Bid two spades (rescue bid). If you have incorporated Jacoby Transfers into your system, obviously you would bid two hearts, thereby transferring into spades.

3. ♠ K J 10 9
   ♥ Q 7
   ♦ A 2
   ♣ Q 10 9 6 2

   Bid two clubs. If partner bids two spades, you will raise to four spades. Over anything else, you will bid three no trump.

42

4. ♠ K 9 2   Pass.
   ♥ J 6 3
   ♦ 10 9 8 7
   ♣ Q 5 4

5. ♠ K 6 2   Invite to three no trump by
   ♥ Q 4 3   calling two no trump.
   ♦ J 9 8 6 4
   ♣ Q 5

6. ♠ K 6 4   Four no trump. This invites
   ♥ A 6 3   partner to bid six no trump
   ♦ K J   if he is maximum.
   ♣ K J 10 9 6

7. ♠ K Q 9 4 2   Two clubs asking for a
   ♥ Q 8 6 3   major. If partner bids one,
   ♦ 10 4   then you should pass. If part-
   ♣ 9 6   ner bids two diamonds, you
                  will bid two spades (promis-
                  ing a five-card suit). Partner
                  might raise two spades be-
                  cause this is an invitational
                  sequence.

8. ♠ K 7 4   Two no trump. You have
   ♥ J 10 6   seven high-card points and a
   ♦ Q J 10 8 7   five-card suit.
   ♣ 9 2

9. ♠ 2   Four hearts—quick before
   ♥ K Q 8 7 the opponents bid spades.
        6 4 3 2 However, if you are now
   ♦ 5 4 2   playing transfer bids, then
   ♣ 9   you should bid two dia-

43

monds and raise partner's two hearts to four. This last sequence may not be quick enough to keep the opponents from bidding spades.

10. ♠ 2
♥ K 3
♦ Q J 9 8 6
   5 4 3 2
♣ 10

Bid five diamonds and hope partner's points are in the right spots—like aces instead of kings.

In the following cases, partner has opened two no trump. What is your response?

11. ♠ 7 6 2
♥ 10 9 7
♦ Q 8 4
♣ J 10 3 2

Bid three no trump. You know you have at least 25 points and maybe 27. There's no guarantee here, but you've got to try it.

12. ♠ K 7 5 2
♥ Q 4 3 2
♦ 7 5
♣ 10 8 5

Bid three clubs to ask for a major. You must test it out.

13. ♠ 2
♥ 9 8 5 4 3 2
♦ 10 3 2
♣ 7 6 4

Pass if you're not playing transfers. Bid three diamonds and pass partner's three hearts if you are.

In the following case, partner has opened three no trump. What is your response?

14. ♠ A 10 3 2
    ♥ J 9 7 3
    ♦ 4
    ♣ 9 8 4 3

Pass. You need not look for a major. Partner has enough cards to make three no trump with this dummy. Besides, what are you going to bid if you try Stayman and partner doesn't have a major?

3
SHALL WE PREEMPT?

"Preemptive bids are the spice of life at the bridge table. When properly used, they will often frustrate your opponents and get you a great result; in addition, the preemptor's partner will be well placed to assess his side's offensive and defensive potential. Occasionally preempts will backfire and your opponents will get the good result; but if a little risk-taking isn't part of your arsenal, stick to a crossword puzzle. Preempt often and have fun!"

Betty H. Bender

Preemptive bids are such fun, and so very frustrating to the opponents! Maybe that's why we all have a feeling of fiendish glee when our weak hands happen to be the preemptive type, and weak as they are, we can still take action with them and make life hard for the opposition.

You remember that a high-level opening bid of a suit is made on a hand not nearly strong enough to open the bidding at one. For heaven's sake, don't bid three of a major suit if you can bid four. Don't bid three or four of a minor suit if you can bid five! You are describing your hand on this bid; you've said it *all*, and you will never speak again. So it's important that you let your partner know exactly what you have. You *must* have a seven-card suit.

47

You will decide how many to bid according to whether or not you are vulnerable. If you are not vulnerable, count the number of tricks your hand will take and bid three more than your hand will produce. If you are vulnerable, you can afford to be set two tricks, so bid only two more than you can make. You fully expect your opponents to double you, and you hope they will—rather than be able to ʰⁱd the game they almost certainly have.

Here's a hand that's a good illustration of a preemptive bid:

♠ K Q J 9 8 7 5 4 This hand will never take a
♥ 2   trick unless you play it in
♦ 6 3   spades. If you do, you expect
♣ 10 2   to take seven tricks. So, if
                   you're not vulnerable, bid
                   four spades. If vulnerable,
                   bid three spades.

The partner of the preemptor must not raise voluntarily just because he has a "good" hand. He must have enough quick-taking tricks to ensure that partner will make his bid instead of going down—plus another one for the raise.

Here's an example:

♠ 10 2   This hand has a lovely 13-
♥ K Q 6 4   count in high cards and
♦ Q J 10 6   would have opened the bid-
♣ A J 10   ding, but he should most cer-
                   tainly *pass* his partner's
                   three spade open. Now, if the
                   opponents should get into

48

the bidding, he *should* raise his partner, but never unless he has to compete.

Here's another freak hand that you should be eager to bid:

♠ 4
♥ Q J 10 9 8 7 5
♦ 5
♣ A 4 3 2

This hand should open four hearts if not vulnerable and three hearts if vulnerable. At first glance it would seem that there are only six winners, but we generally consider the fourth card in another suit to also be a winner. So let's be an optimist and bid four hearts.

Here is the partner of the four-heart bidder:

♠ Q J 6
♥ K
♦ K Q J 8
  7 4 3 2
♣ 6

He would have made a preemptive diamond bid if he had dealt, but he must *not* bid his suit now because his partner has said loud and clear that his hand is worthless unless played in hearts. So, this hand will pass and hope to be helpful. But you can see that the king of hearts is his only contribution.

There is a bid that some of you may not know about or use, but it is a very popular way to be as preemptive as possible on a poor hand. It is called the "weak two bid." If you and your partner decide to use this bid, you must realize that you forego the opening two bid with a very strong hand which forces the game and hopes for a slam. However, those enormous hands occur so seldom that many people have decided to use the two-club bid as the *only* forcing-to-game bid. If you do this, two diamonds is partner's response showing less than seven points. Then opener will bid his real suit, whatever it may be, and the partnership will proceed on to game.

If you play the weak two bid, there is a lot of preemptive value in a bid of two spades, two hearts, or two diamonds—and the weak two bid is the answer to those weak hands when your suit has only six cards, since the preemptive three and four bids require a seven-card suit.

Here is a hand to consider:

♠ K J 10 9 8 7
♥ 3
♦ 9 6
♣ Q 10 6 2

You are not vulnerable. You have only six high-card points, but the weak two-bid range is between six and eleven points. Open two spades. If you are not playing weak two bids, you must pass.

Here's a similar hand:

♠ 6 3
♥ Q J 10 9 7 6
♦ A 2
♣ 10 9 8

If you are not vulnerable, open two hearts. You expect to go down three tricks. If vulnerable, you will just have to pass.

50

Here's a hand that's a little different:

♠ A 8 6
♥ J 9 8 7 5 2
♦ 4
♣ K 7 6

This hand would seem to qualify for a weak two bid. You have a six-card suit and eight high-card points, but your suit is too weak. You pass.

If the partnership decides to adopt the weak two bid, let's take a look at how partner should respond.

Here's your hand:

♠ 6
♥ K 8 5 3
♦ 10 7 3
♣ A 7 6 4 2

Your partner opened two hearts and the opponent passed. You immediately bid three hearts which makes the bid even more preemptive!

Let's look at another one:

♠ A 4
♥ A 8 5 2
♦ 8 3
♣ K Q J 9 6

After partner's two-heart opening bid, this hand looks like a good possibility for game, doesn't it? You bid four hearts.

Sometimes when partner opens a weak two bid, you won't be sure whether or not the combined hands are good enough for game. To raise to three does *not* invite game. It's preemptive, too, as we saw in a previous hand. So bid two no trump to investigate. If the opener is weak, he will rebid three of his suit and partner will, of course, pass. But if he has more

51

than a minimum (as much as eight or nine high-card points), he will bid some other suit where he has some values.

Let's take a look at partner's hand:

♠ A K 3	After the opening bid of two
♥ A 8 5 2	hearts, this hand would bid
♦ 6 4	two no trump. If opener just
♣ Q 10 8 3	bids three hearts, this hand
	will pass.

Here is the opening two heart hand:

♠ 8	When his partner bids two
♥ K Q 10 6 4 3	no trump after the opening
♦ 7 5 3	bid, this hand now bids three
♣ K J 4	clubs as he has nine high-
	card points and some club
	values.

The partner who bid two no trump is delighted to hear the club bid and he will now bid four hearts. Look at the two hands and you will see that they'll make four easily. This is a very important bid to remember if you and your partner decide to incorporate the weak two bid into your system.

Let's look at a hand where the partnership is using the weak two bid. We will bid the hand and then play it.

NORTH
- ♠ K 8 7
- ♥ 8
- ♦ K Q J 10 6 4
- ♣ K 10 7

WEST
- ♠ 5
- ♥ A K 5 2
- ♦ 9 8 3 2
- ♣ 9 6 5 4

EAST
- ♠ J 6 2
- ♥ Q J 10 9 6
- ♦ A 7
- ♣ A J 2

SOUTH
- ♠ A Q 10 9 4 3
- ♥ 7 4 3
- ♦ 5
- ♣ Q 8 3

Bidding:

SOUTH	WEST	NORTH	EAST
2 spades	pass	2 no trump	pass
3 clubs	pass	4 spades	pass
pass	pass		

West leads the king of hearts. When dummy goes down, he switches to the five of spades. Declarer takes the ace in his hand. *Don't* ruff a heart in dummy at this point. You need the entry for those diamonds. Instead, lead the five of diamonds. East takes the trick with the ace and leads another trump. Be sure to take it with the queen in declarer's hand, and then lead a trump to dummy's king and pitch your losers on all those diamonds.

Let's see now how in the world we shall cope with our opponent's preemptive opening bid. An opponent's opening bid of three or four is the most maddening thing that can happen to you when you are sitting there with a beautiful hand and so little bidding space. Everybody at the table knows the opener is very weak, but that doesn't make your problem much easier to solve.

Your opponent has opened three spades. Here is your hand:

♠ 6
♥ A K Q J 8 7 5
♦ A Q 6
♣ 4 2

This is a beauty. Only five possible losers, so, of course, you bid four hearts and you don't even care if your partner is dead.

Here's another hand. The opponent has opened three spades:

♠ 7 2
♥ A K 8 7
♦ A Q J 3
♣ K Q 10

You most certainly want your partner to bid, don't you? How you proceed depends entirely on what system you choose to play. Some people like the Fishbein Convention to force partner to bid over a preempt. Others like the Cheaper Minor Convention. Still others bid three no trump to make the partner bid. If you use Fishbein or the Cheaper Minor, your bid on this hand is four clubs.

54

This forces partner to bid his suit, just as a take-out double does. If you happen to subscribe to three no trump, then bid it. This also forces partner to bid his suit. In all of these systems, a *double* after a preemptive bid is strictly for penalties and partner has no choice except to pass.

However, I would like to go on record as saying that I *MUCH* prefer the optional double over a preemptive bid! To me, it is infinitely more satisfactory! After all, this is a partnership game, isn't it? I feel that my partner's judgment is as good as mine. So, on this hand, I shall double. I'd like for my partner to bid, but if he decides it will be more profitable to pass and set the opponents, it is most certainly his privilege. Whatever he chooses to do is absolutely all right with me. Whatever system you and your partner decide to adopt will be fine as long as you both understand it thoroughly, but I strongly recommend the optional double.

I'm sure you are all aware of the fact that the preemptive overcall is made on exactly the same hand that would open with a preemptive bid, and you count your winners the same way, determining the number you bid by your vulnerability.

Here's an example:

♠ K 2
♥ 6
♦ K Q J 10 9 4 3 2
♣ 7 5

The opponent opens the bidding with one spade, and this hand, not vulnerable and in second position, should bid five diamonds. (You will notice that I'm optimistic enough to count on taking a trick with the king of spades.) There's always the possibility that the opponents will bid five spades, but at least you're making it tough for them—which is all you can do. So be sure to do it at every opportunity.

Test Yourself

You are the dealer and are vulnerable. What do you bid on the following hands?

1. ♠ 6
   ♥ A K Q J 7 5 4
   ♦ 8 7 5 2
   ♣ 2

Three hearts. You can't be set more than two tricks.

2. ♠ Q J 10 9
       6 5 3 2
   ♥ 9
   ♦ A 7 3
   ♣ 6

Three spades. You should take seven tricks.

3. ♠ 7 6
   ♥ 3
   ♦ A Q J 9 8
     5 4 3 2
   ♣ 2

   Four diamonds. Don't even consider bidding less. The opponents could easily bid four of a major anyway, but make it hard for them.

4. ♠ 8 7
   ♥ K Q J 10
     7 6 3 2
   ♦ 3
   ♣ 6 5

   Three hearts. You expect to be set two tricks.

5. ♠ K 6
   ♥ 4
   ♦ 9 3 2
   ♣ K Q J 8 5 3 2

   Three clubs. Minor suits are not nearly as hard for the opponents to cope with, but you have to try.

6. ♠ K J 10 9
     8 7 6 5
   ♥ 2
   ♦ 10 7
   ♣ 6 4

   Horrible, isn't it? But you'll have to bid three spades.

You have dealt. You and your partner are playing the weak two bid. What do you bid if you're not vulnerable?

7. ♠ 6 3
   ♥ K Q 10 7 6 3
   ♦ K 5 4
   ♣ 9 8

   Two hearts.

8. ♠ A J 10 7 3 2
   ♥ K 6
   ♦ A 4 3
   ♣ 3 2

   One spade. Plenty strong enough to open the bidding with one.

9. ♠ 7   Two diamonds. A perfect bid
    ♥ 8 2   for this weak hand.
    ♦ K Q J 5 4 3
    ♣ 6 5 4 2

10. ♠ Q J 10 7 5 3   Two spades, of course.
    ♥ 6 2
    ♦ K 7 3 2
    ♣ 2

11. ♠ 3   Three hearts. Don't open
    ♥ K Q J 10 7 6 4   this at two, as the hand will
    ♦ 4 2   take too many tricks for
    ♣ 6 5 3   that. You'll be down three at
                         three hearts.

4
WHAT'S FORCING?

" 'What's forcing?' is one of the most important nuts and bolts aspects of the game of bridge. When you and your partner have a firm agreement about what bids are forcing and what bids guarantee that partner will have another chance to speak, your partnership is on solid ground. 'Almost' and 'usually' will only undermine your partnership—bids are either forcing or they're not. Make your agreements and don't fudge!"

Betty Ann Kennedy

To play bridge well, you must know which bids are forcing and which ones aren't. You must recognize a forcing bid from your partner, and you must know when your hand justifies a forcing bid and be sure to make it. When your partner makes a forcing bid and you have a dreadful little minimum hand, you may wish you could quietly crawl off someplace—but you don't have that option! In fact, you have *no* option as long as you are being forced. Trust your partner and do your duty, and he will do the same for you!

Anytime the partner of the opening bidder changes the suit, the opener is absolutely forced to bid again. The only exception to this is if the partner has previously passed. But, even in this case, the opener

59

should most certainly *want* to bid again.

OPENER		PARTNER	
♠	A 9 7	♠	8 2
♥	K J 8 4	♥	Q 9 5
♦	A 2	♦	K 10 9 7 6
♣	Q 10 8 3	♣	J 4 2

The opener bids one club and his partner responds one diamond. The opener must bid again, so he bids one heart. Now the partner with his minimum hand will pass, as opener's bid of another suit at the one level doesn't promise any additional strength.

Here's another forcing situation:

OPENER		PARTNER	
♠	A 9 7	♠	8 2
♥	K J 8 4 2	♥	Q 10 9 5
♦	A 2	♦	K Q 10
♣	Q 10 9	♣	A J 7 6

The opener bids one heart and partner bids three hearts, a jump raise showing good four-card heart support and opening strength. This is a definite force to game. So the opener bids four hearts.

Now we have a hand that makes the strongest of all forcing bids—the jump shift.

OPENER		PARTNER	
♠	A 9 7	♠	K Q J 10 6 5
♥	K J 8 4	♥	A 9
♦	A 2	♦	K Q J 7
♣	Q 10 9 3	♣	2

The opener bids one club and partner bids two spades (bidding one more than necessary in another suit). The jump shift bidder should have 19 points and either very good support in his partner's suit or a self-sufficient suit of his own. This bid forces to game and is a very strong invitation to slam. The opener now bids three spades, and partner bids four no trump, asking for aces. The opener bids five hearts, showing two aces, and since there is an ace missing, the partner bids six spades.

Let's look at a hand in which the jump shift must be a "made-up" bid, because there is no biddable suit in which to jump. It's always wise to jump shift in a minor suit in a case like this instead of a major.

OPENER	PARTNER
♠ A 9 7	♠ K Q 10
♥ K J 8 4	♥ Q 9
♦ A 2	♦ K Q 7
♣ Q 10 9 3	♣ A K 8 7 2

The opener bids one club. Not having a real suit of his own, partner jump shifts by bidding two diamonds, to tell his partner he hopes for a slam.

An opening bid of two in a suit (playing the American Standard System) is forcing on the partnership to game.

OPENER	PARTNER
♠ A K J 10 7	♠ 9 6 3
♥ A K Q J 8 4	♥ 10 2
♦ 2	♦ J 10 7 3
♣ 9	♣ 8 6 3 2

61

The opener bids two hearts and his partner bids two no trump (showing fewer than seven points). The opener then bids three spades, and the partner, who *must* keep bidding until game is reached, bids four hearts knowing from the bidding that the heart suit is longer.

Here we have a hand in which the opening bidder makes the jump shift.

OPENER	PARTNER
♠ KQJ106	♠ 843
♥ AQ	♥ J82
♦ 2	♦ A10954
♣ AQ1054	♣ J2

Bidding:

OPENER	OPPONENT	PARTNER	OPPONENT
1 spade	pass	1 no trump	pass
3 clubs	pass	3 spades	pass
4 spades	pass	pass	pass

Anytime the opener rebids in a new suit by jump shifting (bids one more than necessary), it is a force, and partner may not pass until game has been reached. Opener should have 21-22 points.

Now here is an example of bidding that I'm afraid many players don't realize is forcing—or sometimes choose to ignore as forcing. So I would like to really emphasize this: When the responding hand bids at the two level over his partner's open and the opener's next bid is *anything* except a rebid of his suit, it is

100 percent forcing, and the responding hand absolutely *must* bid again.

OPENER		PARTNER	
♠	A 7	♠	4 3 2
♥	K Q 8 6 4	♥	A 9
♦	A 10 9 8 4	♦	J 7 3
♣	2	♣	K Q J 9 6

Bidding:

OPENER	OPPONENT	PARTNER	OPPONENT
1 heart	pass	2 clubs	pass
2 diamonds	pass	?	

This one is a little tough. Responder doesn't want to bid no trump with nothing in the spade suit. Rebidding clubs would be an exercise in futility. So it looks like the lesser of evils is to bid two hearts, as much as he hates to do it. At least they'll still be at the two level. The only thing absolutely certain about this hand is that he *can't* pass.

Let's look at four hands this time, bid them, and then play the hand.

NORTH
♠ 6
♥ 10 9 6 3
♦ A 8 7
♣ K Q 10 4 2

WEST
♠ K J 7 5 3 2
♥ K 7
♦ 2
♣ 9 8 6 5

EAST
♠ A 10 9
♥ Q 2
♦ K 10 9 6 5 3
♣ J 7

SOUTH
♠ Q 8 4
♥ A J 8 5 4
♦ Q J 4
♣ A 3

Bidding:

SOUTH	WEST	NORTH	EAST
1 heart	1 spade	2 clubs	2 spades
pass	pass	3 hearts	pass
4 hearts	pass	pass	pass

You will notice that the opener passed the second round because East's two spade bid kept the bidding alive for opener's partner, and a pass showed him that it was a minimum open. When partner raised to three hearts, opener decided to bid four. Though he was not forced, his partner showed him a good hand with heart support. The opening lead was the two of diamonds. Declarer should be very suspicious

64

of that lead, when the opponents had bid and supported spades. So he very quickly took the trick with
the ace in dummy. He then led a trump from dummy
and did *NOT* finesse. After taking the ace of hearts,
he led a small one, and luckily the king and queen
fell together. So, no problem!

Here are two hands that will be fun to discuss:

	OPENER		PARTNER
♠	QJ1086	♠	K732
♥	K4	♥	A5
♦	AQ92	♦	6
♣	K7	♣	AJ10862

Bidding:

OPENER	OPPONENT	PARTNER	OPPONENT
1 spade	pass	2 clubs	pass
2 diamonds	pass	3 spades	pass
4 spades	pass	4 no trump	pass
5 diamonds	pass	6 spades	pass
pass	pass		

When the opener bids one spade, partner *knows*
the hand will be played in spades. He counts his
points and gets 17 (promote the king and promote
the singleton). We all know that a jump raise or a
jump to two no trump over partner's open takes 13-15
points. So, this hand is too good for that. He bids
two clubs (which is forcing for one round) and then
jumps in spades next time, which describes his hand
perfectly to his partner. If he had forgotten to promote
he would have had just 15 points. Now they can go
on and bid their slam

65

Here is another hand:

♠ 8
♥ A Q J 6 3 2
♦ K 8 4
♣ A J 9

You open the bidding with one heart, and after any response from partner, you jump to three hearts. This is *not* a forcing bid, but it shows a good suit and high hopes for game.

With any of the following hands, partner should raise to four hearts:

♠ A 6 4 2	♠ K J 6 5	♠ Q 7 6 3
♥ 9 4	♥ 10 9 5	♥ K 4
♦ A 6 5	♦ Q 3	♦ 6 5 2
♣ 10 4 3 2	♣ Q 6 3 2	♣ K 10 7 4

But if he had this hand, he should pass:

♠ K 7 3 2
♥ 7
♦ Q 7 5 2
♣ Q 4 3 2

Here is a hand where the opener jumps in partner's suit:

66

OPENER	PARTNER
♠ A J 10 8	♠ Q 7 6 4 3
♥ K Q 8 3 2	♥ J 9
♦ A Q 4	♦ K 6 3
♣ 3	♣ K 10 4

Bidding:

OPENER	OPPONENT	PARTNER	OPPONENT
1 heart	pass	1 spade	pass
3 spades	pass	?	

The three-spade jump is not absolutely forcing. It shows great support in partner's suit and 18-19 points. With 20 points, opener would have bid four spades. This is a strong request for partner to bid four if possible—and with the hand above, I think he should, though there is a possibility it will go down. Always remember that opener's jump raise to four in his partner's suit shows more strength than bidding three. In other words, even if the responder has a minimum hand, he knows there should be a game!

Sometimes good contracts are missed because one or the other of the partnership didn't make a forcing bid when he could have, so his partner didn't fully realize the strength of the combined hands. Be sure to describe your good hands when you're lucky enough to have them.

Test Yourself

I have opened the bidding with one spade. What will I do with this hand after the following responses from partner?

1. ♠ A J 10 8 5
   ♥ K 7 3
   ♦ Q 8 5
   ♣ K 2

(a) One no trump?   (a) This is not forcing—so I pass my minimum hand.

(b) Two spades?   (b) This is also not forcing—so I pass.

(c) Two clubs?   (c) I rebid two spades, showing a minimum hand.

(d) Two hearts?   (d) This is forcing once, so I bid three hearts.

(e) Two no trump?   (e) This is also forcing, so I bid three no trump.

My partner opened one heart and I bid two clubs. What is my action after partner's rebid as follows?

2. ♠ K 3
   ♥ Q 7 6
   ♦ 10 9 5
   ♣ K Q 10 7 4

(a) Two diamonds?   (a) I bid two hearts—a preference.

(b) Two hearts?   (b) I pass. He is minimum—no game!

(c) Three clubs?

(c) This is forcing, so I bid three hearts.

(d) Two spades?

(d) A reverse bid showing a very strong hand. I bid three hearts.

(e) Two no trump?

(e) I have no trump distribution so I bid three no trump.

Partner has opened one club. What is my response? Why?

3. ♠ Q 10 7
   ♥ K 3 2
   ♦ 7 4
   ♣ J 10 7 3 2

Two clubs—because it is the only bid I have. You would never bid a no trump on this hand, because a no trump response over a club bid promises 10 points. The reason for this is that a minimum responding hand has so many choices over one club. He may bid one diamond, one heart, or one spade, or raise the club.

4. ♠ K Q J 10 7 3
   ♥ K J 10
   ♦ A K 5
   ♣ 2

Two spades—a jump shift demanding game and hoping for a slam—because I have 19 points and a splendid suit.

5. ♠ K 10 7
   ♥ A 2
   ♦ Q 6 4
   ♣ A J 10 7 3

Two no trump—a force to game showing opening strength. I'd rather try to make three no trump than five clubs.

6. ♠ A 10 7   One diamond, with the plan
   ♥ 6   to jump in the club suit later.
   ♦ K Q 2   I had to make up a bid at this
   ♣ A 10 7 6 5 2 point, as I'm too strong for
                 just a three-club immediate
                 raise.

7. ♠ Q 6 5   Pass and hope the opponents
   ♥ Q 3 2   are dumb enough to pass too.
   ♦ 8 4 3   There is nothing else in the
   ♣ 7 4 3 2   world I can do.

5
OVERCALLS, ETC.

"The first bid by your side after your opponents have opened the bidding is an OVERCALL.

"Getting your side into the bidding is important for several reasons: You may bid and make a contract your way; you may have a good sacrifice; you may push your opponents too high; or you may indicate a good opening lead to your partner. An overcall has a general nuisance value, as it uses up your opponents' bidding space and makes it harder for them to bid accurately.

"The requirements to overcall are quite liberal, depending on the LEVEL OF BIDDING and the VULNERABILITY, so you will have plenty of opportunities to bid."

Wm Root

When you overcall, you know that your opponent who has opened the bidding has a pretty good hand. So with mediocre holdings, you should be careful—because the remaining strength is divided beween opener's partner and your partner, and who knows which one has the most? The first thing to remember when you make an immediate overcall in a suit is that your suit should be healthy. One of the reasons you overcall is to suggest an opening lead to your partner should he have the lead. So you wouldn't want to bid a suit if you'd be embarrassed to have it lead to you. Also, you don't want to lose more than two tricks in your overcall suit. The point count of your hand may vary from about nine points up to 17 when you overcall at the one level, and your partner will surely count on your having a good five-card suit.

We'll look at some hands and decide what we'll do with them. If you think your hand will produce four tricks, it's worth a bid at the one level.

Your opponent has opened one club. Here is your hand. What will you do?

♠ 4 2	You have eight high-card
♥ 8 6 5	points and that doubleton
♦ A K J 10 3	makes nine. So vulnerable or
♣ 10 6 5	not, you should overcall one diamond.

The opponent opens one heart. What is your decision with this?

♠ K 10 9 8 7	This is a ten-point hand, and
♥ 9 6 3	I consider the suit good be-
♦ 8 2	cause of those body cards
♣ A Q 10	(10, 9, 8, and 7). So, you should overcall one spade.

The opponent bids a diamond. Solve this problem!

♠ 5 3	I have just said you should
♥ A K J 10	have a five-card suit to make
♦ 7 6 4	an overcall! But this four
♣ A J 6 5	card suit is so *good* that you should bid one heart any- way.

The opponent bids one club. What will you do with this beauty?

♠ 7   This is a magnificent hand,
♥ A Q 10 6 4   but there is nothing that you
♦ K 8 3   can do with it except bid one
♣ A K 8 2   heart.

When you make an overcall at the two level, your hand must be better. You should be able to take five tricks in your hand, though you need not have many high-card points. Just as at the one level, you must have a good suit.

Consider the next two hands. Your opponent opened with one heart. What should you do?

♠ 4 2   This is a great suit and a good
♥ 7 6   hand. You would happily bid
♦ K Q J 9 7 5   two diamonds—vulnerable
♣ A 10 8   or not!

♠ K 2   Your diamond suit isn't so
♥ A 3   hot, is it? But not vulnerable,
♦ Q 10 8 5 4 2 you'd bid two diamonds—
♣ 9 6 5   though, if you were vulnera-
                ble, you'd pass.

Here's a hand that I imagine people will disagree on. The opponent bid one spade. What do you think?

73

♠ 6 4
♥ A Q 10 5 3
♦ K Q 9
♣ 7 5 2

This hand would be a great one-level overcall, but good as it looks, it could be very dangerous at the two level. So, just pass it.

Here, the opening bid is the same, and if you'll notice, the cards are too—except they are rearranged.

♠ 6
♥ A Q 10 5 3
♦ K Q 9 4 2
♣ 7 5

What a difference distribution makes! Of course, you'd bid two hearts because if you're unlucky enough to get doubled, you'd have a great escape hatch! You could then bid three diamonds.

Your opponent opens one spade. Just look at this hand.

♠ A J 10 8 2
♥ 7
♦ A Q 9 4
♣ K Q 3

It's absolutely gorgeous, but the only thing in the world you can do is *pass*.

The opponent opens one no trump and here is your hand:

♠ 7 2
♥ K J 9 8 4
♦ A Q 4 3
♣ K 5

This is a very handsome hand, but you should pass. The best time to overcall a no trump is when you have a *long* suit and a very distributional hand.

I find that a great many people are uncertain about what to do when partner has overcalled. You have several choices. With as few as seven points and support in his suit, raise him. Remember, your trump support doesn't have to be as good to raise an overcall as it should be to raise an opening bid. Why? Because you know the overcall suit is a good one, and we open the bidding with very poor suits sometimes. When you open, the count in the hand matters. When you overcall, the strength of the suit matters. If you can't raise your partner's suit, you may have a suit of your own to bid—or perhaps you could bid no trump.

We'll look at some hands and see what to do with them. With the next three hands, opener bids one club, partner bids one spade, and the opponent passes.

♠ K 6 3
♥ 8 3 2
♦ A 10 7 4
♣ 9 8 6

You have spade support and seven points, so you will raise partner to two spades.

♠ J 9 5
♥ A K 4 2
♦ A 8 7
♣ 10 5 3

Your 12 lovely points are enough to raise partner to three spades. This is not forcing and, if he's minimum, he will pass.

75

♠ Q 6 3 2	An enormous hand, and you
♥ A 7 4	certainly want to force part-
♦ A Q 9 8 5	ner to bid game. So you cue
♣ 8	bid two clubs. If you prefer
	to just bid four spades, I
	won't quarrel.

The opponent opens one heart, partner bids two diamonds, and the opponent passes. This is a tough one. What will you do?

♠ A K 8 4	You have 10 beautiful high-
♥ 6 2	card points, so you must do
♦ K 9	something. You certainly
♣ 10 7 6 5 3	can't bid spades or clubs, and
	since your partner's overcall
	was at the two level, he must
	have a good suit. So, you
	have no choice but to bid
	three diamonds—even with
	the doubleton.

The opponent opens one spade, partner bids two hearts, and the opponent passes.

♠ 6 5 3	With your excellent trump
♥ J 7 4 2	support and all those high
♦ A Q 10 9	cards, you should make
♣ A 4	game. So bid four hearts.

We'll look at some hands now that illustrate when you'd make a bid of your own over partner's overcall.

The opener bids one club, partner bids one diamond, and the opponent passes.

♠ 7 5 2
♥ A J 10 6 4
♦ K 8 6
♣ 5 3

You have a good five-card major suit and should bid it rather than raise partner's diamonds. Bid one heart.

On this same hand, partner overcalls one spade over the one club bid.

♠ 7 5 2
♥ A J 10 6 4
♦ K 8 6
♣ 5 3

Now we have a very different situation. You should always bid a major instead of raising a minor—but you should raise your partner's major instead of bidding the other major. Bid two spades.

The opener bids one club, partner bids one heart, and the opponent passes.

♠ 8 7 3
♥ 6 2
♦ A Q 9 5
♣ K 10 4 3

You have nine high-card points and should not pass partner's overcall. Clubs are well stopped, so you should bid one no trump, which describes this hand nicely.

The bidding on this next hand is the same. The opener bids one club, partner bids one heart, and the opponent passes.

♠ A 5 3 2
♥ J 4
♦ Q 10 9 7
♣ A Q 10

You have 13 high-card points and should certainly bid two no trump. If partner has a minimum overcall, he will bid three hearts and then you must pass.

77

We have talked about no trump opening bids, so we needn't spend too much time on no trump over-calls because the requirements are exactly the same. If the opponent opens the bidding with one suit and you have no trump distribution and no trump count—including very *good* stoppers in the oppo-nent's suit—you overcall one no trump.

The opponent opens one heart. Here is your hand:

♠ K 10 3   You have no trump distribu-
♥ A J 10   tion and 17 points. So you
♦ K Q J 7 2   bid one no trump.
♣ K 5

Your partner will treat your bid exactly as if it were an opening no trump—raise if he can, pass if he must, or rescue to a long suit if he's very weak and distributional.

The same is true of preemptive hands. We've talked about opening with a preemptive bid, and the overcall requirements are just the same.

The opponent has opened the bidding with one diamond. Here is your hand:

♠ K Q J 9 8 7 5 2   If you are not vulnerable,
♥ 8 3   you will overcall four
♦ 2   spades. If you are vulnerable,
♣ 7 4   you will bid three spades.

I'll wind up my discussion of overcalls by talking about another type that I feel is so very important and, oh, so useful! Unfortunately, many players over-look this golden opportunity to get into the action, and I hope very much that you won't! Suppose the

78

bidding goes like this: Opener bids one club, partner passes, and the opponent passes. Here's your hand:

♠ K J 6
♥ K J 9 8 7
♦ J 10 9 3
♣ 2

It certainly isn't anything to shout about, is it? But there is certainly something very wrong with this bidding. The partner of the one club opener couldn't even scare up six points to respond, so the cards must be some where, and the chances are very good that we have more of them than they do. I wouldn't want to overcall on this scraggly little hand in second position, but I wouldn't miss the chance for the world in fourth position. I bid one heart, as I wouldn't dream of letting them get a little part score without a fight. This is reopening the bidding—or "balancing"— as the bidding would have been all over if I had passed. I hope you will remember this and do it whenever you have a chance. You'll be glad you did!

Test Yourself

In each of the following examples, your opponent on your right opens one heart. What is your call?

1. ♠ K 4
   ♥ A J 6
   ♦ K J 7 5
   ♣ A J 10 6

   You will bid one no trump. You have no trump distribution, stops in the heart suit, and 17 points.

2. ♠ K Q J 10 6 5
   ♥ 9 3
   ♦ 6 2
   ♣ 10 9 8

   You will take five tricks with this hand, so be as big a nuisance as possible and bid two spades.

3. ♠ 9 3
   ♥ A 2
   ♦ K Q J 9 5 2
   ♣ 7 6 4

   This hand is certainly good enough to overcall at the two level, so you bid two diamonds.

4. ♠ Q 10 4
   ♥ K 6 4
   ♦ 8 2
   ♣ A 10 9 6 5

   This hand is too weak to enter the fray. Just pass.

5. ♠ K 6
   ♥ K 10
   ♦ Q 8 4
   ♣ A K Q J 7 5

   With six lovely club tricks, you'd surely overcall one no trump. Even though you do not have no trump distribution, you have 18 high-card points and expect to make one no trump.

6. ♠ K Q 10 9 8
   ♥ J 4 3
   ♦ K 6
   ♣ Q J 5

You have a good suit and enough strength for a one-level overcall. Bid one spade.

7. ♠ K Q
   ♥ A 6
   ♦ Q 10 8 7
   ♣ Q 10 6 4 3

Even though this hand has 13 points, there is no proper action to be taken. So it will pass.

8. ♠ K Q 10 8 6
   ♥ 5 4 3
   ♦ J 6
   ♣ K 8 3

This is a scrawny little hand, but you'd still overcall one spade because it has a decent suit.

The opponent has opened the bidding with one spade. What is your call?

9. ♠ 10 6 4 3
   ♥ A Q J 10 5
   ♦ K 10 2
   ♣ 6

Some players would no doubt pass this hand, but the suit is good and the distribution is good. You'd bid two hearts.

10. ♠ 2
    ♥ A 2
    ♦ 10 7 4 3
    ♣ K Q J 7 6 2

This is a healthy two-club bid—a fine suit, a singleton in the opponent's suit, and an ace.

11. ♠ Q J 2
    ♥ K J 5 3 2
    ♦ A 4 3
    ♣ Q J

What do you have here? A 14-count hand, but it could be a real disaster if you even think of bidding. *Pass!*

12. ♠ 10 9 6 2   Two hearts, of course! This
     ♥ A Q 10 9 8 3 hand meets the require-
     ♦ K 3   ments for a two-level over-
     ♣ 5   call (vulnerable).

13. ♠ A 2   Be brazen and bid two hearts
     ♥ 10 9 8 7 2   *only* because you have a
     ♦ A K Q 10 4   good diamond escape hatch
     ♣ 3   in case you get a double. The
                  opponents may well bid four
                  spades. If so, you can't help
                  it.

6
DOUBLE VISION

"When an opponent has opened the bidding, you should usually pass. Much more often than not, one of the opponents will become declarer in such cases; and any action by you will help declarer by telling him where most of the missing high cards are.

"If you have a good hand and a strong suit of five or more cards, however, you may accomplish something worthwhile by bidding your suit. Perhaps you can play the hand; or your bid may steer your partner to a favorable opening lead.

"If you have good support for all of the unbid suits, you should consider doubling any low bid when your turn comes. This tells your partner, 'I think this hand belongs to us rather than to the opponents. However, I don't know which suit should be trumps. *You* make that choice. Don't pass my double, because I'm so short in their suit that they'll probably make their doubled contract against us.'

"This kind of double, known as a *take-out* double, is one of the most useful of all bidding weapons *provided it is used properly.* If you watch this program, you'll have no trouble learning when to double and how to respond to your partner's double."

Alfred Sheinwold

I'm sure you will never play bridge for two or three hours without several take-out doubles being made at the table. It's a very potent weapon in this game, and everyone at the table needs to know what to do after a take-out double. Before we look at some hands and discuss them, let's review for a moment exactly what the player needs to have to make a good, sound, immediate take-out double:

1. You promise not more than two cards in the opponents' suit.
2. You promise opening bid strength (a minimum of 13 points).
3. You promise support in both major suits if you double a minor.
4. You promise *good* support in the other major if you double the opponent's major.
5. You promise *much* more strength than the minimum if you double and then later bid your own suit.
   NOTE: You should not double if your hand has two suits. You would like to bid them both, so just overcall and hope you'll have a chance to bid the other suit later.

If your opponent opens the bidding with one spade, what should you do in the following cases?

♠ 5 3 2
♥ K Q 8 4
♦ A 9 6
♣ K J 7

This is a perfectly good 13-point hand, isn't it? But you have three little cards in the opponent's suit, so you shouldn't double. Just pass.

84

♠ 5 3 2
♥ K Q 8 4
♦ A Q 6
♣ A J 7

Here is a lovely 16-point hand with no trump distribution, but you have nothing in the spade suit. So you can't bid no trump. By the same token, those three little spades keep the hand from being a good double. You must pass.

♠ 5 3
♥ K Q 8 4 2
♦ A 9 6
♣ K J 7

This is a very iffy sort of hand. Your heart suit isn't so great, but if you're absolutely dying to bid, you might bid a sketchy two hearts. Otherwise, the better part of valor would be a pass.

♠ 5 3
♥ K Q J 4 2
♦ A 9 6
♣ K J 7

I'm sure you have noticed how very similar all of these hands are. This one is a good two heart bid. However, it is not strong enough to double first and then bid. So just bid two hearts.

♠ 5
♥ K Q 10 4 2
♦ A 9 6 3
♣ K J 7

On this hand, you would double the opponent's spade open. But if he had opened one club or one diamond, you would bid one heart.

♠ 5 3
♥ K Q 8 4
♦ A 9 6 3
♣ K J 7

No problem here. You double.

♠ 6	Again, a perfect double over
♥ K Q 8 4	the one spade. But you
♦ A 9 6 2	would pass over any other
♣ K J 7 3	opening bid.

♠ 5	This hand has great shape for
♥ Q J 8 4	a double, but it is much too
♦ Q 9 6 2	weak. You pass.
♣ K J 7 3	

♠ K Q 10 5 3	With this hand you pass
♥ 4	with glee, and just hope the
♦ K 9 6 2	opponents will play the hand
♣ A J 7	at one spade.

Your opponent opens one heart. What should you do?

♠ A K J 9 7 2	You will double with this
♥ 8	beauty of a hand. After part-
♦ A Q 6	ner's response, you will bid
♣ K 3 2	your spades, which will tell
	him how very good you are.

Your opponent opens one heart. What should you do?

♠ A K J 4	You have three little cards
♥ 8 3 2	in your opponent's suit
♦ K Q 10	which, as I said, makes a
♣ A Q 6	double a no-no. Even though
	you have 19 lovely high-card
	points, just pass.

Now let's talk about what the partner of the opening bidder should do after the opponent makes a takeout double. Here are some general guidelines.

- With a bad hand and poor trump support—pass.
- With a good hand—10 points or more—redouble.
- With trump support for partner—aggressively raise.
- With a fair hand but no trump support—bid a suit or no trump.

Let's decide what to do with the following hands if partner opens one heart and the opponent doubles.

♠ 5 3 2
♥ 8 4
♦ J 8 5 3
♣ Q 6 4 2

This is a bad hand—with no support for partner's suit. You pass.

♠ 5 3
♥ Q 8 4
♦ J 8 5 3
♣ 7 6 4 2

This is a pretty sad looking hand, isn't it? But you have support in partner's suit, so bid two hearts! This may keep doubler's partner from bidding.

♠ 5
♥ Q 8 4 3
♦ K 8 5 3
♣ 7 6 4 2

Now the hand is looking considerably better, so bid three hearts. Your partner knows you're not really good or you would have redoubled. This three-heart bid makes it very difficult for the opponents!

♠ 5
♥ Q 8 4 3 2
♦ K 8 5 3
♣ 7 6 4

This hand should bounce right into four hearts if you are not vulnerable. If you had a void in spades, you would bid four, even if vulnerable.

♠ K Q J 5 3
♥ 8 4
♦ J 8 5
♣ 7 6 4

This hand could well bid one spade. If you would prefer to pass in hopes that the opponents will bid a spade, it would be okay.

♠ 5 3
♥ 4
♦ J 10 8 5 3 2
♣ Q 6 4 2

With the singleton in your partner's suit and such a bad hand, bid two diamonds. You do have six of them.

♠ 5 3
♥ 4 2
♦ J 10 8 5 3
♣ Q 6 4 2

Pass. You now have no reason to speak!

♠ 5 3
♥ Q J 8 4
♦ K 9 8 5
♣ A 6 4

With this nice hand, you redouble—planning to raise your partner's hearts next time.

♠ 5 3
♥ Q J 8 4
♦ A 8 5
♣ A 6 4 2

Redouble—and on your next bid you will *jump* raise your partner's hearts.

♠ K J 8 4	This hand will, of course, re-
♥ 5 3	double. His thinking is very
♦ A K 8 5	different this time, as he
♣ 6 4 2	hopes to double the oppo-
	nents and set them at spades
	or diamonds.

I want to point out here that the opening bidder should pass after his partner redoubles and let the redoubler take charge of the hand. The opener can't know, at that point, whether it will be better to play the hand or set the opponents. So he should let his redoubling partner decide.

Now we will move around the table and sit in the seat of the doubler's partner. He has important decisions to make, so let's see how he will do it. Here again we have some general guidelines to help us.

When partner has made a take-out double, he should proceed as follows:

- With 0-7 points—overcall.
- With 8-10 points—jump the bid.
- With 11 points or more—cue bid.
- With very strong trumps in the opponent's suit and a good hand—pass.
- *Never* pass from fright! The worse your hand is, the more important it is to bid.

Your opponent bid one heart, your partner doubled, and the right hand opponent passed. What do you do?

♠ 6 5 3 2	Just be very thankful that
♥ 8 5	you happen to have four
♦ J 10 5 4	spades and need not bid at
♣ 8 7 4	the two level. Bid one spade.

89

♠ Q 5 3 2
♥ 8 5
♦ J 9 5 4
♣ K 7 4

This hand is considerably better than the last one, so you are much happier to bid one spade.

♠ Q 5 3 2
♥ 8 5
♦ K 9 5 4
♣ K 7 4

Now things are looking up. You have eight high-card points and a doubleton. So you must tell partner. Bid two spades.

♠ Q J 5 3 2
♥ 8 5
♦ K 9 5 4 2
♣ 4

Again, a nice hand opposite a double. Nine points in all, so you bid two spades.

♠ Q 5 3 2
♥ 8 5
♦ K 9 5 4 2
♣ K 7

A good hand with eight high-card points and two doubletons. You have a fine two spade bid.

♠ 5 3
♥ 9 8 5 3 2
♦ J 5 4 2
♣ 7 3

A terrible hand but you must bid two diamonds.

♠ 5 3
♥ Q 10 5 3 2
♦ J 4 2
♣ 7 5 3

Another terrible hand, but you must bid something, so bid two clubs. When your long suit unfortunately happens to be the suit the opponent has bid, you must make the cheapest bid possible in a three-card suit. In other words, if this hand had con-

90

tained three cards in the spade suit, the bid would have been one spade.

♠ 5 3
♥ Q J 10 8 2
♦ K 4 2
♣ 7 5 3

With this hand you would pass for penalties. You and your partner can probably set one heart.

♠ Q 5 3 2
♥ 8 5
♦ K 9 5 4
♣ K 7 4

This hand is still worth a jump and you must tell your partner. So, you bid three spades.

The opponent opened one heart, partner doubled, and opener's partner raised to two hearts. What will you do with the following hands?

♠ 6 5 3 2
♥ 8 5
♦ J 9 5 4
♣ 8 7 4

You pass, and are very happy not to have to bid with this miserable hand.

♠ Q 5 3 2
♥ 8 5
♦ J 9 5 4
♣ Q 7 4

You'd be much happier if you could bid one spade, but your partner is still eager to hear from you, and you won't let the pesky opponent keep you from bidding. Bid two spades.

♠ Q 5 3 2
♥ 8 5
♦ K 9 5 4
♣ K 7 4

You will notice that this is exactly the same hand you held previously when the opener's partner did not raise him, and you jumped to two

91

spades. Well, this hand is still worth a jump and you must tell your partner. So, you bid three spades.

Many times the doubler's partner is a little too timid about bidding. Remember, without even a face card in your hand, you are forced to bid when partner doubles and the opponent passes. So when your hand is better than seven points, be sure to tell your partner about it! Jump!

Another little tidbit to tuck away in the back of your mind is the fact that the doubler is often too optimistic. Remember that when you make a take-out double you are promising your partner a hand with opening bid strength. So, unless you have quite a bit more than the minimum 13-15 points, you should forever hold your peace after doubling. If you raise your partner or bid yourself, you are showing additional strength.

So, a general sort of rule of thumb is for the doubler to "cool it" and for his partner to be more aggressive.

Test Yourself

Your opponent opens the bidding with one spade. What do you do?

1. ♠ 7 2   Double—a classic example.
   ♥ K Q 10 8
   ♦ A J 6
   ♣ K 10 4 3

2. ♠ 7 2　　　　　Pass. Your hearts are not
　 ♥ K 10 8　　　good enough.
　 ♦ A Q 7 6
　 ♣ K J 10 3

Partner opens one spade. The opponent doubles. What do you do?

3. ♠ 10 9 7 2　　Bid two spades. Try to make
　 ♥ 8 6　　　　it difficult for the opponent
　 ♦ A 8 6 3 2　to bid.
　 ♣ 6 4

4. ♠ 6 3　　　　Bid two spades. You know
　 ♥ 10 9 7　　　your partner realizes you
　 ♦ Q 3 2　　　don't have much. You didn't
　 ♣ K J 10 8 4　redouble. But your bid may
　　　　　　　　discourage the opponents.

Partner opens one heart. The opponent doubles. What should you do?

5. ♠ A J 7 4　　Redouble to show your 10
　 ♥ 8 2　　　　points. You do not promise
　 ♦ K 10 5　　heart support when you re-
　 ♣ Q 10 3 2　double.

6. ♠ Q 7 6　　　Pass, because you have no-
　 ♥ 5 4 2　　　thing to say.
　 ♦ J 8 3
　 ♣ J 10 9 5

The opponent opens one heart. Partner doubles. The opponent passes. What will you do?

7. ♠ 9 8 6 2   You bid one spade.
   ♥ Q J 10 3
   ♦ 4 3 2
   ♣ 8 5

8. ♠ K J 10 3   You bid two spades.
   ♥ 10 9 6 4
   ♦ A 9 7
   ♣ 8 2

9. ♠ K 10 9 8   You bid two hearts—a cue
   ♥ A 6 3 2   bid showing a great hand.
   ♦ K Q 4
   ♣ 5 3

10. ♠ 9 8 3   You bid one no trump. You
    ♥ Q J 10 8   have the opponent's heart
    ♦ K 9 7   suit and scattered values.
    ♣ J 5 4

7
DOUBLE DOUBLE VISION

"Even if your partner has opened the bidding and you have a fairly good hand, you can't get rich doubling an opponent at one or two of a suit. If the opponent's partner has support for the doubled suit, he'll make his contract; and then you'll discover that your side should have played the hand at some other suit. If the opponent's partner doesn't have support for the doubled suit, he'll bid something else, and then your prey will escape.

"Most experts use doubles of very low contracts to show strength and length in unbid suits.

"If your partner opens the bidding with one of a suit, and the next player bids one of a higher suit, your double doesn't mean: 'Please pass, partner. We're going to collect a fortune.' Instead, it means: 'Please try something else.'

"Of course, if the opponent makes a *high* bid after your partner has opened the bidding, you may wish to double for penalties. Therefore you and your partner should agree on when a double is for penalties and when it is meant to be taken out. This program will tell you what you and your partner should agree upon in this delicate situation."

Alfred Sheinwold

We've already talked a lot about doubles, and there's a lot more talking to do. Believe me, we haven't even scratched the surface with this fascinating and important phase of the game of bridge.

When there's a take-out double at the table, all four players must figure out how to proceed. So, let's consider what the doubling hand will do on the next round.

Here's the hand:

♠ K J 8 4
♥ 5
♦ A 10 3 2
♣ K J 6 3

Bidding:

OPPONENT	YOU	OPPONENT	PARTNER
1 heart	double	pass	1 spade
pass	?		

What do you do? At the risk of sounding like a broken record, you should pass—pass—*pass!!* You have told your partner you'll be happy with anything he bids—and you are! You have told him you have opening bid strength—and you do. Do you have anything else to offer? The answer is, of course, no!

I don't know why it is that some doubling partners have a go-to-pieces when they hear a bid from partner which pleases them, and feel called upon to raise! Please don't! You have exactly what you promised— no more—so a pass is the clear answer! Any further action you take promises additional values, doesn't it?

One important thing to remember that some players might not think of is that when you double, your partner will be the declarer; so you should count your hand as dummy (which is what you will be). This means that your singletons will count three points instead of only two, and a void suit will count five points instead of three! (You know, of course, the doubleton does not change in value. It counts only one point.) Be sure to tuck this fact away in the back of your mind because it may make a great big difference in how you bid.

Here's the hand:

♠ K J 8 4
♥ 5
♦ A K 3 2
♣ K J 6 3

Bidding:

OPPONENT	YOU	OPPONENT	PARTNER
1 heart	double	pass	1 spade
pass	?		

Now the situation is very different. You *do* have additional strength, so you should tell your partner that you're better than the minimum take-out double by bidding two spades.

Now, on these following hands the bidding has gone:

OPPONENT	YOU	OPPONENT	PARTNER
1 heart	double	pass	2 spades
pass	?		

♠ K J 8 4	This is still a minimum dou-
♥ 4	ble, but your partner has
♦ A 10 3 2	jumped to two spades. So
♣ A 8 3 2	you raise him to three spades
	and leave the decision of
	whether to go on or stop to
	him.

♠ K J 8 4	This is a good double, so
♥ 4	when partner jumps to two
♦ A 10 3 2	spades you may certainly bid
♣ A Q 3 2	four spades.

♠ K J 8 4	You are delighted that your
♥ 4 2	partner could bid two
♦ A 10 3 2	spades, but you are too weak
♣ A 8 3	to speak again. So, please
	pass!

There are so many valuable uses of the take-out double—and some of them are sometimes overlooked. Suppose you have this hand:

♠ K J 7 4
♥ Q J 10
♦ 9 7
♣ K 10 9 3

Bidding:

PARTNER	OPPONENT	YOU	OPPONENT
pass	1 diamond	pass	2 diamonds
pass	pass	?	

What will you do now? You have the same weak little hand you started out with—but things are different now! The opponents don't sound so great, do they? A raise of the one diamond bid is music to your ears! Now is the time to get into action! You should double—and your partner will not be fooled for a minute, as he realizes that you've passed originally. See if you can perhaps get a small part score— or maybe chase them up high enough to set them! Don't miss an opportunity like this when it comes your way!

Here's another opportunity some players may overlook because they get discouraged too easily.

Here's your hand:

♠ A Q 10 4
♥ K Q J 6
♦ 6
♣ A Q 8 3

Bidding:

OPPONENT	YOU	OPPONENT	PARTNER
1 diamond	double	2 diamonds	pass
pass	?		

So, it's up to you again—and, of course, you will *double* again! This tells your partner you're absolutely loaded and he *must* bid—no matter what!

Here's another case where you're more than justified in forcing a weak partner to bid.

Here's your hand:

♠ A Q J 7 3
♥ K Q 10 2
♦ 6
♣ A J 6

Bidding:

YOU	OPPONENT	PARTNER	OPPONENT
1 spade	pass	pass	2 diamonds
?			

You must double to tell your partner that this hand belongs to your team, and you have no idea of letting the opponent "steal" it! He must bid!

This is used as a take-out double but some players don't know about it. It's very vital, so don't forget it.

Here's a very interesting hand. This situation comes up fairly often, so it's very important to know how to handle it.

♠ K 10 8 4
♥ Q J 10 9
♦ A 6 2
♣ J 2

Bidding:

OPPONENT	PARTNER	OPPONENT	YOU
1 diamond	double	pass	?

What a golden opportunity! When partner doubled the one diamond bid, he promised the major suits, didn't he? So, how do you know which one to bid?

You don't! You can ask your partner to choose which major and also tell him about your very nice hand with one simple little bid! The cue bid of two diamonds will get the job done! Pretty neat! And he will know that your side probably has a game.

Sometimes when you open the bidding, you find yourself in a terrible predicament!

Here is your hand:

♠ K 10 7
♥ K Q 6
♦ A 10 9 5
♣ Q 8 4

Bidding:

YOU	OPPONENT	PARTNER	OPPONENT
1 diamond	double	pass	pass

What a dreadful state of affairs! You are just as sure as the doubler's partner is that you'll be set! There's no chance in the world of making one diamond when doubler's partner passes, thus converting the take-out double to a penalty double! Fortunately, there's an escape hatch! You redouble! This is a real SOS saying, "Partner, we're in deep, deep trouble, but anything you bid will be better than this one diamond doubled contract!" Be *SURE* that your partner understands this SOS!

There is another type of double that perhaps you are not familiar with, but it is very popular with good players and widely used. It will be interesting to talk about it, and you may decide whether or not you wish to incorporate it into your system of bidding—whether you do or whether you don't, it's good to know about it. It's called the negative double and is used when your partner has opened the bidding and the opponent has made an immediate overcall.

Let's look at some hands and see how this works.

♠ K 9 5 2
♥ 4 3
♦ 5 3 2
♣ A 8 3 2

Bidding:

PARTNER	OPPONENT	YOU	OPPONENT
1 heart	2 diamonds	?	

If the opponent hadn't overcalled two diamonds, you would have been happy to respond one spade to your partner's opening bid—but now you are without a bid! Very sad! However, if you use the negative double, you will double at this point. This says to your partner, "I can't bid, but I have some values in the two unbid suits. How about you?"·

Here's another hand—similar, but much stronger:

♠ K Q 5 2
♥ 4 3
♦ 5 3 2
♣ A K 3 2

Bidding:

PARTNER	OPPONENT	YOU	OPPONENT
1 heart	2 diamonds	?	

Your first thought when partner opens is that your side will no doubt have a game. This is a great hand, but you can't bid no trump with three small diamonds, and you can't raise partner. What will you do? Double!

Another example with the same bidding:

♠ 8 7 5 2   Couldn't be easier—it's a
♥ 4 3   *pass!* You're much too weak
♦ 5 3 2   to do anything else.
♣ K 9 3 2

When you're playing the negative double, how do you know how much to bid after your partner doubles? You ask yourself what you would have done if the opponent hadn't overcalled. You pretend that your partner responded and proceed as though he had.

Let's take this hand for instance:

♠ A 7 4 3
♥ A K J 5 2
♦ 6 4
♣ 6 4

Bidding:

YOU	OPPONENT	PARTNER	OPPONENT
1 heart	2 diamonds	double	pass
?			

Now bid two spades, just as you would have done if your partner had responded one spade over your opening bid. Remember, his double tells you he has values in the two unbid suits.

103

Here's a hand with the same bidding:

♠ A 7 4 3
♥ A K J 5 2
♦ 6 4
♣ A 4

Now, if your partner had made a normal spade response over your opening bid, you would have given him a jump raise with this very good hand. So you do the same over his negative double. Your bid is three spades.

This hand is even better! Same bidding.

♠ A J 4 3
♥ A K J 5 2
♦ 4
♣ A 5 4

Now, you are really loaded and partner's negative double is sweet music. You have 20 points (don't forget to count your singleton three points even though you'll play the hand—to all intents and purposes, your partner has bid the spades by his double). So, you can now happily bounce into four spades. But there's one other alternative. If you and your partner want to be fancy, you can cue bid the diamonds; however, I'd suggest that you keep it simple and bid four spades.

Don't forget for a minute that if you decide to use the negative double, you may no longer double your opponent's overcall for penalties! When the opportunity comes, you'll just have to grit your teeth and pass. You can't have it both ways, so you'll have to make up your mind which will be more valuable to you. If you opt to incorporate the negative double into your system, there's always a chance that your partner may reopen the bidding by doubling—which would be a mighty happy circumstance.

For instance, your partner has this hand:

♠ A 7 4 3
♥ A K J 5 2
♦ 4
♣ 6 4 3

Bidding:

PARTNER	OPPONENT	YOU	OPPONENT
1 heart	2 diamonds	pass	pass
?			

You were loaded in diamonds and know you could set the opponent, but you couldn't double for penalties because you and your partner are playing the negative double. So, suppose your partner now doubles to reopen the bidding. Happy day, you can pass and set the contract!

With this hand, partner couldn't double. He would just reopen by bidding two hearts:

♠ A 4 3
♥ A K J 10 5 2
♦ 4
♣ 6 4 3

105

Bidding:

PARTNER	OPPONENT	YOU	OPPONENT
1 heart	2 diamonds	pass	pass
2 hearts			

There's a lot to think about and a lot to learn about all types of doubles Every time you play bridge, there will be take-out doubles, penalty doubles, negative doubles.... You name it, you'll have them!

Here's an example of the sort of hand you dream about (and the opponent has nightmares about)!

```
                    NORTH
                  ♠  9
                  ♥  K J 6 3
                  ♦  A Q J 4
                  ♣  A J 8 2

     WEST                        EAST
  ♠  5 4                      ♠  A Q 10 6 3
  ♥  10 9 8 7                 ♥  Q 5 4
  ♦  K 5 3                    ♦  10 8 2
  ♣  9 6 5 3                  ♣  K 7

                    SOUTH
                  ♠  K J 8 7 2
                  ♥  A 2
                  ♦  9 7 6
                  ♣  Q 10 4
```

Your partner is north. The bidding:

NORTH	EAST	SOUTH	WEST
1 diamond	1 spade	pass	pass
double	pass	pass	pass

You and your partner have agreed to use the negative double, so you must pass the opponent's spade overcall, even though you know you can set him. Your partner, who opened, has a beautiful take-out double which is music to your ears. Now you gleefully pass, converting it into a penalty double. The poor opponent may be able to salvage three tricks from this fiasco—but, of course, this sort of thing doesn't happen too often.

Test Yourself

You and your partner are using the negative double. Partner opens one spade, and the opponent bids two clubs. What do you do?

1. ♠ 8 7 3
   ♥ K 10 5 4
   ♦ Q 7 6 3
   ♣ K 8

   This is a golden opportunity to tell your partner you have something in the other two suits and see if he has, too. Double.

Partner opens one club and the opponent bids one spade. What is your call?

2. ♠ 10 2
   ♥ K Q 10 5
   ♦ K 7 3 2
   ♣ 6 5 2

   You double to see if partner has anything in hearts or diamonds. If so, he will bid them.

107

You have opened one diamond, the opponent over-calls one spade, partner doubles, and the opponent passes. So, now it's your turn again. What will you do with the hands below?

3. ♠ 7 3
   ♥ A 6 5 2
   ♦ A K J 7 3
   ♣ Q 10

You will bid two hearts and your partner will pass, un-less he has more than the minimum for a negative double.

4. ♠ A K 2
   ♥ 10 9 5
   ♦ A K J 9 8
   ♣ Q 10

On this hand, since you don't have four cards in either unbid suit, but you *do* have 17 points, you would bid two no trump, as you know your partner's points are mainly in hearts and clubs.

Partner opens one spade and the opponent over-calls two diamonds. What is your call?

5. ♠ 8
   ♥ K 10 9 8 6 3
   ♦ Q 10 8 4
   ♣ 7 6

Pass. If your partner doubles, you will bid two hearts (you are too weak to hope to set them). If your partner rebids two spades, you'll just have to pass.

6. ♠ Q 6
   ♥ K 8 4
   ♦ Q 10 8 4
   ♣ K J 7 3

Pass. You hope your partner will reopen with a double, so can pass and set them.

7. ♠ 8 7
   ♥ K Q 10 9
   ♦ Q 10 8
   ♣ Q 6 3 2

Double. This is a perfect negative double.

Partner opens one club and the opponent overcalls one spade. What is your call?

8. ♠ 7
   ♥ K 10 9 6
   ♦ Q 8 4 3
   ♣ K 6 3 2

Double. Of course you have a great club raise for your partner, but if you do that you might miss a fit in the heart suit.

9. ♠ J 3 2
   ♥ K 10 6 3
   ♦ Q J 8 4
   ♣ Q 4

Double. Be happy that you are using the negative double, because otherwise you could never speak.

8

COMPETITIVE BIDDING

"Competitive bidding is to bridge what putting is to golf—it separates the winners from the losers."

Bobby Wolff

This one short but potent statement from our superstar, Bobby Wolff, certainly tells it like it is. I wish I'd thought of that comparison myself.

Competitive bidding is where the fun is! That's what this game is all about! The battle is joined with no holds barred! Each team eagerly tries to outbid the other—or push the others up high enough so they'll get set—or scheme to take a small, harmless set themselves to keep the other team from scoring big below the line! Each hand is an exciting contest! Let's take a look at some hands and try to figure out our very best bet on each one.

Some hands are good for offense only and some have a lot of defensive strength. So, it's pretty important to think in terms of the potential value of your hand from both angles when the bidding gets spirited.

Here's a hand to think about:

♠ VOID	This hand is absolutely great
♥ 6 5	for offense. It will probably
♦ K Q J 9 8 6 4	take six diamond tricks and
♣ Q J 10 7	maybe a couple of clubs, but
	if the opponents win the
	contract, I wouldn't count
	on taking a single trick.

Here's a hand that is wonderful defensively. You'd much rather try to set the opponents with this hand than to make a contract yourself.

♠ A 7 6	Those two lovely aces and
♥ K Q J	the king-queen-jack will
♦ A 6 3	produce a lot of tricks
♣ 7 5 3 2	against any contract.

Sometimes there is a question in your mind as to whether to double the opponents or to pass when the bidding gets high and you're pretty sure of setting them. For goodness' sake, *don't* double if, by locating the strength in your hand, you could help them make their bid.

Here's a hand that illustrates this point:

♠ 9 6 2
♥ K J 6 4
♦ A 3 2
♣ J 8 4

112

Bidding:

OPPONENT	PARTNER	OPPONENT	YOU
1 heart	1 spade	2 diamonds	pass
2 hearts	pass	4 hearts	?

If you double four hearts, they will finesse you like mad. But if you sit tight and don't give the show away, you'll have a real good shot at setting them! Pass!

Here's another hand that takes some careful thinking in order to decide what's best:

♠ 7
♥ K Q 10 5 2
♦ A Q 8 6
♣ A 4 2

You have dealt and you open the bidding with one heart. Your opponent overcalls one spade and you are delighted when your partner jumps to three hearts. But now the overcaller's partner bids four spades. What to do? You know from the bidding (the fact that you have opened and your partner has shown opening strength by his jump raise) that your side has the big cards and that this hand belongs to you. Your partner is well aware of this, too, so you should *pass* and leave the decision up to your partner. He will decide whether it would be more profitable to bid five hearts or double and set the opponents. This is a *forcing pass* and your partner absolutely must take some action. The only thing he cannot do is pass.

Here is a hand that has the same bidding:

♠ 7
♥ A K 10 8 6 3
♦ 6
♣ K J 9 8 7

You open one heart. Your opponent overcalls one spade. Your partner jumps to three hearts and the same nuisance of an opponent bids four spades. The bidding is back to you, and this time you have no problem! You will bid four no trump hoping your partner has two aces. If he does, you'll bid six hearts. If he has only one ace, you'll bid five hearts.

Here's another hand with the identical bidding as the last two:

♠ K 10 5
♥ A 9 8 6 4
♦ K J 4
♣ A 7

What will you do this time when the opponent comes forth with his four-spade bid as before? This looks to me like the time to double! This is a partnership game, remember? And your partner may decide to bid more if he

114

wishes, depending on what his hand looks like.

Many hands at the bridge table are played at less than game contracts. So we are very often faced with a part score situation. Either we have a part score or the opponents do, and this state of affairs most certainly affects our bidding. It makes for fiercely competitive action! The side with the part score is eager to complete a game, and the other team is just as determined to prevent it if at all possible!

We'll look at three hands. In each case, you have dealt and the opponents have a part score. What should you do?

♠ K J 10 7 2
♥ A 8 3 2
♦ Q 9 6
♣ 4

This is certainly a very sketchy little hand, isn't it? You don't have the count for an opening bid, and you surely don't have two defensive tricks. It's a sub-par hand in every respect. So what will you do? You will open this hand one spade! In a situation like this, thievery is legal, and this is the time to try to steal!

♠ A 10 4 3
♥ K Q 6 5 4 2
♦ 8 3
♣ 4

Here is another questionable hand. If your team was the one with the part score, you'd pass this. But since the opponents have the part score, you most certainly would open the bidding with

115

one heart and be happy to do it.

♠ A Q 9 6 5
♥ 9
♦ K J 4 3 2
♣ 8 3

This hand isn't so great in the defensive trick department, is it? In fact, it's a very iffy little hand. But, since you have dealt and the opponents are the ones with the part score, I think you might well open this hand one spade.

Remember, when the opponents have a part score, you *want* to bid. Some people may not realize this. They get timid and want to pass the hand out. Please don't! When you have a part score, you should have a better hand because you can bet that the opponents will try to push you too high.

Let's look at a hand and decide what to do in various situations. Partner has dealt and passed. The opponent opens one heart.

♠ K Q J 10 8 6 3
♥ 7
♦ J 10 8
♣ 3 2

This hand should make a preemptive overcall of three spades. Partner has passed, so it's obvious that the opponents have all the strength and you must try to keep them from getting to their contract. If your side happens to have a part score, it is especially advantageous to be willing to take a set of 500 points, because you will still have your part score! A sacrifice isn't as advisable when the opponents are vulnerable because you give them all those points above the line, and they're still vulnerable! The time for a sacrifice bid is when they *aren't* vulnerable.

When the competitive bidding gets pretty high and you have a part score, it's better to go on and double the opponents if you're *sure* you can set them than to gamble on a bid you might not make.

It is an amazing and sad thing that many players miss bidding their slams because they happen to have a part score.

Let's look at two hands and see how they should be bid. Here is opener's hand:

♠ 4
♥ A Q J 10 7
♦ A 8 6 2
♣ A Q 8

You have a part score of 60. This is a beautiful hand and opens the bidding one heart.

Partner has this hand:

♠ A 7 5
♥ K 9 3 2
♦ Q 4
♣ K J 6 3

This hand absolutely *must* jump to three hearts—showing great trump support and opening strength.

Now, the opening bidder will just bid six hearts, as he has 17 high-card points and those three lovely aces—to say nothing of a singleton. Unfortunately, some partners might have just raised to two hearts because of the 60 part score.

Balancing, which is getting into the act when it would appear that the opponents aren't very strong, is one of the most important ways of competing—and it is not used enough by some players. Let's look at several hands and decide what to do. You have dealt and passed. The opponent bids one diamond, your partner passes, the opponent's partner passes, and now it's your turn again:

♠ A 10 6 3
♥ Q J 7
♦ 8 6
♣ K 10 7 3

For heaven's sake, don't pass and let them steal this hand. You are as good as they are! *Double* — which certainly won't fool your partner in any way, as you passed originally. He will be very grateful to you for competing!

♠ A 10 6 3 2
♥ Q J 7
♦ 8 6
♣ K 10 7

Same bidding. With this hand, you should bid one spade. You have a five-card suit, so bid it! Remember, spades are golden! There's an old saying that "having spades is worth three points!"

♠ A 10
♥ Q J 7 5 3
♦ 8 6 2
♣ K 10 7

This hand can't double because it's no good in the spade suit, and it contains three diamonds. But it does have a five-card heart suit. So bid it!

118

♠ A 10 6 5 3 2
♥ Q J 7 5
♦ 8
♣ K 10

This hand was a maximum pass in the first place, wasn't it? So now you can afford to double because if partner bids two clubs, you can bid two spades. If partner bids hearts, you might even have a game! All the values in this hand are good.

Let's try another hand. You deal and pass. The opponent opens one spade, partner passes, opener's partner bids two diamonds, and it's your turn again.

♠ 7
♥ K J 6 4 3
♦ 8 5
♣ A Q 8 5 3

You are well aware of the fact that the opponents have the lion's share of the cards—an opening bid and a two - level response — but now is the time to compete! A very effective way to do it is to bid *two no trump!* This is, of course, the unusual no trump, asking partner to bid the longer of two unbid suits. This is such a valuable bid to know about and you'll use it often! For instance, if the opponents bid one spade and then three spades and you bid three or four no trump, you are asking part-ner to bid the longer of his *minor* suits. Anytime it's obvious from the bidding that the no trump bid is im-

119

possible, your partner will know that you are using this very descriptive convention, showing a highly unbalanced hand, with two long suits, and you wish partner to select the one that your team should compete with.

We'll take a look at all four hands and the complete bidding.

NORTH
♠ 7
♥ K J 6 4 3
♦ 8 5
♣ A Q 8 5 3

WEST
♠ K J
♥ A 7
♦ Q J 9 4 3 2
♣ J 9 2

EAST
♠ A Q 9 8 4
♥ Q 5
♦ A 6
♣ K 7 6 4

SOUTH
♠ 10 6 5 3 2
♥ 10 9 8 2
♦ K 10 7
♣ 10

Bidding:

NORTH	EAST	SOUTH	WEST
pass	1 spade	pass	2 diamonds
2 no trump	double	3 hearts	3 no trump
pass	pass	4 hearts*	double
pass	pass	pass	

*I know they can make their bid. We'd better take a sacrifice.

Now let's play this hand and see what happens.

West leads the spade king. Then he switches to the ace of hearts, followed by a small heart. The decision to play dummy's king is obvious, as east would never have doubled the unusual no trump with a singleton. Now, how to proceed? The opponents refused to let us cross ruff, so we must try to set up the club suit with only two chances to trump. We lead the ace of clubs and then lead a small one which we trump—noticing that the nine drops from the west hand. We now trump a little spade in dummy. It's time to take stock now. The opening leader has showed up with the king of spades and the ace of hearts so far, and he bid the diamond suit. So he must have had some honor cards there. So, I don't see how he could possibly have the king of clubs too! What happens if I lead the queen of clubs from dummy? If it isn't covered, I'll let it ride and discard a spade or a diamond. So, we do that and it works. I lead the five of clubs now and trump the opponent's king in my hand. I then lead a small spade, trump it in dummy, lead the good little club, and discard a spade. Then I lead a small diamond from

121

the board up to my king and hope for the best! Happy day! It works and the result is the best of all possible worlds! The doubled contract, a sacrifice against a sure game, *makes!* But, whether we could have made the bid or been set, the set would have been better than letting the opponents make a game.

The moral to this story is that competitive bidding is the exciting part of bridge. Don't make the mistake of being timid and letting your opponents take over. You'll make mistakes—who doesn't? But let's make mistakes of commission— *not* of omission. In other words, compete!

Test Yourself

1. The opponent opens one spade, partner passes, and opener's partner bids two hearts. What do you do?

♠ 6	Bid two no trump. This is an
♥ 8 3	unusual no trump, so part-
♦ Q J 10 9 6	ner must bid the longer of
♣ K Q 7 5 4	his unbid suits.

2. The opponent opens one spade, you pass, opponent's partner bids two diamonds, and your partner bids two no trump which is doubled. What do you do?

♠ 6 5 4 3	This is the unusual no
♥ J 2	trump, so in spite of the dou-
♦ 9 7 5 4	ble, you must bid the longer
♣ Q 10 2	of the unbid suits. Bid three
	clubs immediately to show
	partner a preference.

3. Partner opens one spade, and the opponent bids two diamonds. What do you do?

♠ Q 10 9 3
♥ 9 5
♦ A J 6 4 2
♣ K 9

Bid three spades. Don't be tempted to double the opponent's two diamonds. You have too many spades and your side should have an easy game.

4. The opponent opens one heart, partner doubles, and opener's partner redoubles. What is your bid?

♠ Q 10 7 6 5 2
♥ 7 5 3
♦ VOID
♣ K 10 8 6

Bid four spades. Even if you do go down a trick or two, the opponents surely have a game.

5. The opponent bids one club, partner bids one heart, and opener's partner bids one no trump. What action do you take?

♠ Q J 10 2
♥ Q 10 8
♦ 6 5
♣ J 6 5 3

Not much of a hand, but you should raise your partner to two hearts.

6. The opponent opens one heart, partner bids two spades, and opener's partner passes. What should you do?

♠ A 6 3 2
♥ J 10 7 5 3
♦ 9
♣ 7 6 4

You should make the bid even more preemptive. Bid three spades to make it even harder for opener to find another bid.

7. Partner opens one spade and the opponent bids three hearts. What is your call?

♠ Q 10 9
♥ J 6
♦ A 9 3 2
♣ 7 6 4 3

Bid three spades. The opponent took away your bidding space (as intended). Without the preempt, you would have raised partner to two spades, but your back is against the wall, so compete!

8. Partner opens one spade and you raise to two spades. There are two passes, and the right hand opponent balances with a double. What is your call now.

♠ J 6 5 2
♥ 9 8
♦ K Q 9
♣ K 7 3 2

Three spades. The hand obviously belongs to your side, and you were at the very top of your original raise, so tell your partner.

9. The opponents have a part score and they are vulnerable. You are not. The opponent opens one spade. What is your call?

♠ 6
♥ K Q J 10
    7 5 2
♦ 3 2
♣ J 10 9

Four hearts. Bid the hand to the maximum (and then some) in a situation like this.

9
KILLER HANDS

"Slam bidding is the most challenging aspect of the game. To be good at it, you must adopt some of the popular slam bidding conventions; natural bidding alone will not get the job done. The 'control-showing bid' (often called a 'cue bid') is by far the most useful bid for bidding slams. Other conventions we'll talk about are 'Blackwood,' 'Gerber,' and 'the grand slam force.' You should bid a small slam when you have at least an even chance to make it, but to bid a grand slam, the odds should be two-to-one in your favor. I suggest that you take more chances when you bid a small slam than when you bid a grand slam."

Wm Root

Everybody who plays bridge dreams longingly of getting one of those great, big, beautiful, gorgeous hands that instantly makes visions of a slam dance through the head! Unfortunately, these lovely hands don't come our way often enough; but when they do, we certainly don't want to goof up by not knowing exactly how to handle them, do we?

One way to find out what we need to know from partner is to use the well-known Blackwood Convention. Most players are very familiar with this bid, but just for the record we will go over it briefly. If, from the bidding, it's pretty obvious that you and your partner would like to try to bid a slam, it may be necessary to find out how many aces there are in your two hands. If this is the information you need, you will bid four no trump, which merely asks, "Partner, how many aces do you have?" Partner will answer your question as follows:

- With no aces, he will bid five clubs.
- With one ace, he will bid five diamonds.
- With two aces, he will bid five hearts.
- With three aces, he will bid five spades.
- With four aces, he will bid five clubs.

There is no chance of confusion about whether the five bid means all four aces or none. If you have aces in your hand, his five clubs obviously says he has none. But if you are aceless, you may be sure his five clubs promises all four. After you find out about the aces, *if* you and your partner have all of them, you may want to know how many kings he has. You bid five no trump—and he will answer by the same method.

- With no kings, he will bid six clubs.
- With one king, he will bid six diamonds.
- With two kings, he will bid six hearts.
- With three kings, he will bid six spades.
- With four kings, he will bid six clubs.

We'll look at some hands and decide whether to *ask* for information or whether to *give* information.

Your partner has opened one heart. Here is your hand:

♠ 3
♥ K Q 9 8
♦ K Q
♣ K Q J 10 7 4

What a beauty! All you need to know is how many aces your partner has. So you will bid four no trump.

Your partner's hand:

♠ A 10
♥ A 7 6 4 2
♦ A 10 9 6
♣ A 3

This hand dutifully bids five clubs, showing all four aces. You will then bid seven no trump, knowing that it will be impossible to lose a trick. Wouldn't it be fun to have all of that ammunition!

Here is another hand where the use of the Blackwood Convention is an absolute must.

♠ K Q 10 3
♥ K 4
♦ K Q J 10 5 2
♣ 7

You have dealt and open with one diamond. Your partner responds one spade. You are delighted and jump to three spades. Your partner's bid of four no trump is exciting but, of course, having no aces, you now bid five clubs. Your partner's next bid of five no trump shows you that he has all four aces—because you never ask about the kings unless all aces are accounted for. Your answer of six spades tells

129

him about your three kings—and your partner will undoubtedly bid seven.

Here is another beautiful hand, but one where using the Blackwood Convention would be all wrong! Why? Because there could be a duplication of values. When you have a void, the information you need to get and to give is not the number of aces but *which ones!* Or to be more accurate, you must find out about the "first controls."

♠ A K J 9 7 4
♥ K Q J 2
♦ VOID
♣ A K Q

This lovely hand will open with two spades (the standard American forcing bid) and hears his partner respond with three spades—a positive response showing at least seven points! Obviously, they are slam bound—but how to get there? This is certainly not the time for the Blackwood Convention. Why? Because opener has a void suit, and if partner has one ace it well might be the ace of diamonds, which would not help. So opener will start showing "controls" by bidding four clubs.

Many players either don't know the control-showing bid, or forget to use it, or don't realize its value—but it should most definitely be a part of the bidding system. Remember, the suit must be agreed upon and established in the minds of both partners before

130

either one may launch into a control-showing bid. In this case, the spade suit has been established as the suit for the final contract.

After the four-club bid, if partner should bid four hearts, showing first control in the heart suit, this hand would immediately bid seven spades, knowing the two hands won't lose a trick.

Do not use Blackwood if your hand contains a void.

Let's look at another type of hand in which you'd better think carefully as you try to bid a slam.

♠ A K 10 8 2
♥ 7 3
♦ K 10
♣ A K 9 4

This hand opens one spade and partner gives a jump raise to three spades, showing a hand with *good* four-card support in the spade suit and 13-16 points. So, you certainly have reason to expect a slam, since the total points in your two hands will reach that magic number of 33. However, some of your points are distributional and some of partner's may be, too (singletons or doubletons). So, you need to get specific information about partner's first and second round controls in a suit. Start this information-gathering process by bidding four clubs, to show first round control. And depending on what you learn about

partner's hand, you'll proceed.

*Remember that you should not use Blackwood if
your hand has two quick losers in an unbid suit* (as
the heart suit in this hand).

Here's another hand to consider:

♠ K Q J 7 4 2
♥ K J 10
♦ 4
♣ A 6 3

The bidding is the same.
This hand opens one spade
and partner raises to three
spades. This hand doesn't
quite have enough points to
bid beyond the game level.
You're not sure whether or
not the combined hands
have 33 points. It depends on
partner's hand, doesn't it?
Bidding four no trump would
be too optimistic, and being
willing to settle for four
spades seems a little timid.
So, it looks like a good time
to indicate to partner that
you're interested in a slam.
You do this by showing the
ace of clubs with a four-club
bid. When partner bids four
diamonds or four hearts, you
will just bid four spades.
Partner will get the message
that you're not really sure
about this hand, but the
slam thought has occurred
to you! Now, if partner likes

his hand, he'll just bid six spades. Control showing is an excellent device for investigating the possibilities of a hand.

Here's a hand very similar to the last one, but the addition of the king of clubs makes a big difference.

♠ K Q 9 7 4 2
♥ K J 10
♦ 4
♣ A K 3

When this hand opens one spade and gets a raise to three spades, you *know* that you should have enough for a slam. So, since you don't have a void or a worthless doubleton, bid four no trump. If partner has only one ace, you sign off at five spades. If he shows two aces, you bid six.

We'll look at a hand now as partner of the opener.

♠ K Q 7 4
♥ 6 2
♦ A J 6 5
♣ Q 9 8

Partner opens one spade and this good hand raises to three spades. Now partner bids four clubs and you will bid four diamonds, showing the ace. It is now up to partner.

We've been talking about showing first controls in a suit (an ace, though you may also bid a void suit to show first control); but as the bidding goes on, we may also show second control (which would be a king or a singleton). Let's see how this works.

133

♠ Q J 8 2
♥ A Q 10
♦ K 4
♣ Q 9 6 5

Partner opens one spade, and with this hand you bid three spades. Partner bids four diamonds and you bid your ace of hearts. Partner then bids five clubs. Now, you ask yourself, "What else do I have to offer?" The king of diamonds, of course. Partner has shown the ace of diamonds, so when you bid five diamonds, you are showing the second control.

Let's look at both of these hands together and see how beautifully this bidding works.

OPENER	PARTNER
♠ A K 10 9 6 4	♠ Q J 8 2
♥ K 5	♥ A Q 10
♦ A Q 8 3 2	♦ K 4
♣ VOID	♣ Q 9 6 5

Bidding:

OPENER	OPPONENT	PARTNER	OPPONENT
1 spade	pass	3 spades	pass
4 diamonds	pass	4 hearts	pass
5 clubs	pass	5 diamonds	pass
?			

Now the happy opener will bid seven spades!

If we have been guilty of overlooking this very valuable method of reaching our slam contracts, let's change our ways. Be on the lookout for those hands that require exact information, and be sure to show your controls when it's important. You'll love it!

When your partner opens the bidding and your hand contains 18-19 points, you immediately envision a slam, don't you? With these values, one of the best ways to announce your intentions to your partner is by a jump shift—by bidding one more than necessary in another suit, such as one club-two spades, or one spade-three diamonds. Warning: Be careful about jump-shifting unless you have a fit in your partner's suit or a self-sufficient suit of your own.

Partner opened one spade. Here is your hand:

♠ K J 7 3
♥ 4
♦ A K 9 7 6
♣ A J 10

You will jump shift to three diamonds knowing that you will get to a slam in spades.

Here is another hand with the same opener by partner—one spade.

♠ K 8 6
♥ A J 9 7 6
♦ 6
♣ A K J 8

This hand technically qualifies for a jump shift. You have a fit in partner's suit and a suit of your own, but neither one is spectacular. So, resist the temptation to jump shift and first bid hearts, later clubs. As the bidding goes on, you will find out where the hand should play and will undoubtedly reach a slam somewhere! **NOTE:** Don't forget that for opener to make a jump shift, he must have 21-22 points.

There is a very specialized bid that asks a very definite question, and you may not be familiar with it. It's called the "Grand Slam Force" and, though it comes up very seldom, it's something you should know about.

Here's a hand to illustrate the bid:

♠ Q J 8 6 4   Your partner opens the bid-
♥ A 9   ding one spade. With this
♦ A K Q 9 8 3   hand, what do you need to
♣ VOID   know? *Only* whether or not your partner has the ace and king of spades! You find out by bidding five no trump, which asks, "Partner, do you have two of the top three honors in our suit? If so, bid seven. If you have only one, bid six." There is no possibility of confusing this bid with Blackwood because when using Blackwood you always bid four no trump first.

The opener's hand may look like this:

♠ A 10 9 5 3   He will bid six spades. But if
♥ 7 6   he had two of the top honors,
♦ 5 2   he would bid seven.
♣ A K 8 4

136

I'm sure most of you know and use the Gerber Convention, but our discussion of slam bidding wouldn't be complete without a quick review of the subject.

When your partner bids no trump and you have a big hand with slam possibilities but need to know about aces, you *cannot* use Blackwood because a four no trump response is a raise showing the count of your hand. So, to ask about aces over a no trump bid, use Gerber—which is a bid of four clubs. Partner will answer as shown below:

- No aces—four diamonds
- One ace—four hearts
- Two aces—four spades
- Three aces—four no trump
- Four aces—four diamonds

You will notice that, as in Blackwood, the response is the same for none or all four—but, as in Blackwood, there is no possibility of confusion.

Here's a hand:

♠ K 7 3	Partner opens one no trump.
♥ K Q J 10 9 5 2	This hand bids four clubs. If
♦ A 3	partner shows two aces, this
♣ 2	hand will bid six hearts. If
	he has three aces, you will
	bid seven hearts or seven no
	trump.

It's always fun talking about these big, killer hands; and even more fun when we're lucky enough to have one. Now that we know exactly how to cope with various situations when we're so lucky, here's hoping you'll get these lovely hands soon—and often!

Test Yourself

1. You have opened one heart. Partner responds two diamonds. What is your bid and why?

♠ 2	Four no trump. You only
♥ K Q J 10 6 3	need to know that partner
♦ A K 6 4	has one ace to bid six dia-
♣ A 9	monds.

2. Partner opens one no trump. What is your bid and why?

♠ 2	Four clubs (the Gerber Con-
♥ A 4	vention). You only need to
♦ K Q J 9 7 3 2	know how many aces part-
♣ K 8 4	ner has.

3. Partner opens one heart. What is your bid and why?

♠ A 4	Three clubs—a jump shift,
♥ K J 8 6	as you expect to play the
♦ 3	hand at a slam in hearts.
♣ A K 10 8 6 4	

4. Partner opens one diamond. What is your bid and why?

♠ A K J 9
♥ K J 10 8 5 4
♦ A
♣ J 3

You would not jump shift on this beautiful hand because your heart suit is iffy and you have no fit in partner's diamonds. Bid hearts, later spades, and hope that the bidding will show how to reach a slam somewhere.

5. You have opened one heart. Partner bids three hearts. What is your bid and why?

♠ 2
♥ K Q 10 6 3 2
♦ A K 7
♣ K J 6

The heart suit is now established, so you bid four diamonds, showing first control in that suit.

6. Partner opens one heart. You bid three hearts. Partner bids four clubs. What is your bid and why?

♠ A Q 6
♥ Q J 7 3
♦ Q 10 4 2
♣ K 8

Partner is cue bidding his ace of clubs. Bid four spades, showing an ace.

7. You have opened one spade. Partner bids three spades. What now?

♠ Q J 7 3 2
♥ A K Q 4 3
♦ VOID
♣ A 10 6

You now bid five no trump, asking partner if he has two of the top three honors in spades. If he has both of them, he will bid seven spades. With only one, he bids six.

8. Your partner opens three spades. What do you do?

♠ K 6 5	Bid five no trump. All you
♥ A K J 9 4 3 2	need to know is whether he
♦ A 4 3	has the ace and queen of
♣ VOID	spades.

9. Partner opens two no trump. What do you do?

♠ K J 10 8 6 4 3	Bid four clubs. All in the
♥ 9	world you need to know
♦ K 8 6 3	about is aces. You'll take
♣ 7	your chances on the queen
	of spades.

Partner opens one spade. You respond two clubs and then partner makes a jump rebid of four clubs. There was no bidding by the opponents. What is your call with the following three hands?

10. ♠ A 3 2	Bid four no trump. Partner's
♥ K 10	bid of four clubs indicates
♦ K 10	game even if you have only
♣ A 10 7 4 3 2	ten points. Your controls are
	superb. Bid six clubs if part-
	ner has one ace. If he should
	have none, his answer will
	be five clubs and you would
	pass.

11. ♠ K 10
    ♥ 10 5 2
    ♦ A 8 7
    ♣ A Q 10 5 4

Bid four diamonds. Cue bid your ace of diamonds because slam is a definite possibility, as the king in your partner's spade suit is a key card. Let partner take charge after your four-diamond bid.

12. ♠ 2
    ♥ 10 8 6 3
    ♦ Q J 9
    ♣ K Q J 4 2

Bid five clubs. You may now wish you had bid one no trump over his opening spade, but it's too late. You are forced to game in clubs or spades.

141

10
OPENING LEADS AND LEAD
DIRECTING PLAYS

"I've heard it said, 'Show me a bridge player who always gets off to the best opening lead, and I'll show you a champion.' There's only one thing wrong with that statement: Change the *always* to *usually* and it would be true. The reason is that *no one* can always make the perfect opening lead. It's not an exact science, it's an art.

"Defensive signals are the most important part of being successful after the opening lead. Every card you play can send a message to your partner. Learning to send—and watch for—these messages is a must. If you play a high card, you are encouraging your partner to continue that suit. A low card is discouraging. When you can't follow suit, you should try to tell your partner something about your hand. The discard of a low card in a suit shows you don't have much there. A high card discard is a 'come on.' When following suit, a low card followed by a high one shows an odd number of cards in that suit, and a high card followed by a low one shows an even number.

"Bridge is a lot more fun when you get your signals working for you—and it's really easy!"

If you ask a roomful of bridge players what one single thing about the game gives them the most trouble, I'll bet the answer from the majority would be a booming, thundering cry of, "Opening Leads!"

One player at the table is faced with the problem of making the opening lead on every hand, so it's a responsibility none of us can hope to escape. The opening lead is also a great opportunity—so, instead of thinking of it as something we dread, let's take the positive approach and be *happy* that we have the chance to strike the first blow against our worthy opponents who are trying to make their bid! This very important single play may well decide the outcome of the hand.

Many times people have shown me their hands and asked what they should lead. My answer is invariably, "I have no idea unless you tell me the bidding that has been made at the table." So, when it's your turn to make the opening lead and there has been a lot of bidding, you not only may—but *should*—ask for a review of the bidding if there is any doubt in your mind about who bid what, as it will certainly be important in helping you decide what the very best opening lead will be. Remember, too, that your lead will tell your partner something about your hand, and in this partnership game, it's vital to give all the information—and accurate information—to that person sitting across the table from you!

Let's consider some hands where you get absolutely no clue from the bidding. The opponents have bid one no trump, two no trump, three no trump—so, all you can know is that they expect to take nine tricks at no trump.

Here's your hand:

♠ 8 7 3
♥ J 10 9 6
♦ 10 2
♣ K J 7 3

An easy one! You would never lead from a tenace suit (ace / queen or king / jack) with only four cards in the suit. But you have a lovely sequence, so lead the jack of hearts.

♠ 10 3
♥ Q J 10 6
♦ 7 4
♣ A Q 9 5 4

This hand has a good heart sequence, too, but look at that great five-card club suit. You *do* lead from a tenace against a no trump with as many as five in the suit, so lead the fourth best— the five of clubs.

♠ 7 6
♥ 10 9 5
♦ 10 7 6 5 3
♣ 8 5 2

You'll get hands like this, and all you can hope to do is try to help your partner. Forget the poor little five-card diamond suit and lead the ten of hearts. Your partner will know it's the top of nothing.

♠ 7 6
♥ A 9 7 2
♦ Q 8 7 5 3
♣ A 4

This is a lovely hand, and you have high hopes. Lead your fourth best diamond— the five spot—and with the two aces as reentrys you may take lots of tricks!

145

♠ J 5 3 2
♥ K 10 7
♦ 10 9
♣ A Q 10 2

There's no point in leading a small spade as you don't want your partner to lead that suit back to you. You'd much rather have the heart lead come up to your hand, and you'd never lead from the club tenace with only a four-card suit. So, by the process of elimination, lead the ten of diamonds.

If your partner has bid a suit during the auction and the opponents are playing the hand at no trump, you will almost always lead your partner's suit—the only question is which card. Here are some combinations. Let's underscore the card which should be led.

9 5   10 6 <u>3</u>   Q 6 <u>3</u>   <u>A</u> 7 5   K 7 <u>2</u>
9 6 5 <u>2</u>   J 6 <u>3</u>   <u>Q</u> J 3   <u>Q</u> 2   <u>K</u> 3

In other words, with three cards, lead lowest except when you have the ace. With two cards, lead high. If you have two touching honors, lead high. With four cards, lead the lowest unless you have the ace. If you do have it, lead it.

Sometimes if you have a singleton in your partner's suit and your hand contains an excellent lead, you would ignore your partner's suit, *unless* he doubles the no trump bid.

Here's an example:

♠ 10 6 3 2
♥ 5
♦ 10 9 3
♣ K Q J 7 4

Bidding:

OPPONENT	PARTNER	OPPONENT	YOU
1 diamond	1 heart	1 no trump	pass
3 diamonds	pass	3 no trump	pass
pass	double	pass	pass
pass			

Since your partner doubled the bid, you absolutely MUST lead your five of hearts. If he hadn't doubled, you'd be eager to lead your club suit, of course, and would lead the king (the top of the sequence).

By the same token, if you bid a suit during the auction, your partner doubles the opponents' no trump contract, and you have the opening lead, you MUST lead the suit you bid even though it doesn't look too desirable to you. It's a definite force.

If your partner doubles the opponents' no trump and neither of you has bid a suit, he is asking you to lead the first suit that the dummy hand bid.

While we're talking about leading against a no trump contract, let's quickly go over the old Rule of Eleven that has been in use since the days of whist. When you lead your long suit, be sure to lead the fourth best card. For instance, if your suit is K 7 6 5 4, there is obviously no difference in value of the small cards. But if you lead the fourth best—in this case the five spot—your partner will subtract five from 11 and thus discover that there are only six

147

cards higher than the five spot outside of the leader's hand. He can see dummy's cards and his own, so he knows absolutely how many there are in declarer's hand that are bigger than the five. This can be very helpful, so be sure to always lead your fourth best.

When you lead against the opponents' suit contract, it's a horse of a different color! You know that the chances of taking tricks with small cards in a long suit are practically nil as the opponents will trump. So you must try to get tricks in a hurry. Against no trump with a five-card suit K Q 8 7 3, you would lead your fourth best, but against a suit bid you would lead your king, which will be taken by the ace. Your queen will then take the second trick. If you have A K 9 6 4, you wouldn't dream of leading low, but would open with the king.

Some players are happy as clams when they have a singleton and can hardly wait to lead it. There are times when it is the best possible lead, but there are times when it is very bad. It all depends on what you have in the trump suit.

For instance, if your trump holding is any of these, leading a singleton is a real no-no: 9 7 6 3, K 2, Q 7 5, J 8 4 2. Why? Because your four little trumps will cause declarer a lot of trouble. So don't make it easier for him by using one to ruff. And, in the cases when you have a guarded honor in the trump suit, you'd rather take a natural trump trick.

On the other hand, if your trump holding is any of these, a singleton lead is splendid: A 5, A 4 2, K 5 2, 7 5, 9 6 3. You have trumps to spare with your honors. In the case of the 7 5 and 9 6 3, the little trumps are worthless and it would be joyous to have a chance to ruff with them.

Whenever you have as many as four little trumps in the opponents' suit, the happiest thing that could happen is for declarer to have to trump. So he'd soon be whittled down to your size.

♠	10 6 5 2	Spades are trumps. You'd never lead your singleton. Lead the queen of diamonds, as you have a long suit and *hope* that declarer will soon have to trump diamonds.
♥	8	
♦	Q J 10 7 3	
♣	8 4 2	

Sometimes the most damaging thing you can do to declarer is to open the lead with a small trump. You must keep your ears open to the bidding and your wits about you so that you can recognize the times when a trump lead might be devastating to the opponent.

Here are two sequences of bidding that would make me think it was the perfect time to lead a trump. You and your partner have not bid at all. This is the opponents' bidding:

OPPONENT	YOU	OPPONENT	PARTNER
1 diamond	pass	1 heart	pass
1 spade	pass	3 diamonds	pass
3 no trump	pass	4 diamonds	pass
5 diamonds	pass	pass	pass

If there were *any* possibility of playing a hand at no trump, I can't imagine playing at five of a minor, can you? So you would most certainly think the dummy hand has short suits and is eager to trump. Lead a diamond.

149

Now, suppose the bidding goes like this by the opponents:

OPPONENT	YOU	OPPONENT	PARTNER
1 heart	pass	1 no trump	pass
2 diamonds	pass	3 clubs	pass
3 diamonds	pass	3 hearts	pass
pass	pass		

Your side has not bid and they seem to have a real misfit, with the weak hand which responded one no trump having a slight heart preference. Sounds like a very good time to lead trumps, so dummy can't ruff. Lead a heart.

Here's another example:

DEALER		OPPONENT	
♠ A J 8 7 3		♠ 9 6 2	
♥ K 7		♥ J 10 8	
♦ 2		♦ A Q 9 8 6 5	
♣ K Q 9 6 4		♣ 3	

Bidding

DEALER	YOU	OPPONENT	PARTNER
1 spade	pass	1 no trump	pass
2 clubs	pass	2 diamonds	pass
3 clubs	pass	3 spades	pass
pass	pass		

Obviously, a trump would be a good lead here.

Occasionally, but *very* occasionally, you may decide to lead a trump because, from the bidding, it sounds like the trump suit will be no problem to the opponents and the lead probably won't hurt your partner. Besides, you hate to lead anything else.

Here's a hand.

♠ 9 6
♥ K 10 3
♦ A Q 7 2
♣ K 9 8 5

Bidding:

OPPONENT	YOU	OPPONENT	PARTNER
1 spade	pass	2 spades	pass
4 spades	pass	pass	pass

This is a great hand, and you hope to set the opponents four- spade contract, but you certainly don't want to lead from your good cards. You might be justified in leading a spade to protect yourself, and you don't think it could hurt your partner, who must have a very poor little hand.

If your partner has bid a suit and it's your opening lead against the opponents' suit contract, you would usually lead partner's suit—but you should use your good old common sense. And if there's a better lead, for heaven's sake, make it.

Look at this hand:

♠ 7 3   Partner has bid hearts, and
♥ K 10 8 5 4   with my fistful of them,
♦ 8 3 2   we'll be very lucky if we get
♣ Q J 10   a heart trick. I will certainly

never have another chance to lead, so it would be a lot better to lead the queen of clubs and try to find some tricks for our side against a spade contract.

Opening leads are often a trial, but as you become more experienced they will be less a headache and more a challenge! Remember, nobody's perfect, so just do your best!

As the play of the hand goes on, every card you or your partner play will tell a story. So we try to be alert and give a message or get a message at every opportunity. Suppose your partner leads the king of diamonds against a spade contract.

Here's the dummy hand and your hand:

DUMMY
♠ K 7 6 3
♥ Q 5 3 2
♦ 6
♣ K 8 7 4

YOU
♠ 5 2
♥ A J 10 7
♦ 10 8 7 3
♣ 9 6 2

Your partner was expecting to follow it with the ace, but dummy's singleton changes his mind quickly. It is up to you to give him some guidance on his next lead. Tell him which of the other suits you prefer. If you play a high diamond on his king, you are saying you'd like the higher ranking of the two remaining suits. A small diamond suggests that he lead the lower ranking. He needs your help so give it to him! This comes up very frequently at the bridge table and is a useful thing to know about. Play the eight of diamonds to ask for a heart lead.

Here's another one:

DUMMY
- ♠ K 7 6 3
- ♥ Q 5 3 2
- ♦ 6 4
- ♣ Q 8 4

YOU
- ♠ 5 4
- ♥ K 7 6 4
- ♦ J 10 9 7 5
- ♣ 9 2

I suppose the old "high-low" play is used more often than any signal. Your partner leads the king of clubs and dummy goes down. When you see the queen in dummy, you know your partner has the ace. You have a doubleton club, so, of course, you play your high one—the nine of clubs. When he then leads his ace and you play low, he knows you can trump, so he leads a club the third time.

Along that same line, if your partner leads a suit and the ace is played from the dummy hand, you must tell him whether you want him to play that suit next time he has a chance. A high card says, "Please do," and a low card says, "No thanks."

153

Let's look at just one suit when you have a chance to direct your partner's future lead and must be sure to do it. Your partner opens with the jack of spades.

Here are dummy's spades: Here are your spades:

♠ K 6 4   ♠ A 8 2

The four is played from dummy. Of course, you must not play your ace, but you must tell your partner you have it by playing the eight spot and not the two. Declarer will take the trick with the queen, but your partner knows that when he later leads his ten, the king in dummy will be taken by your ace.

I'm sure that all bridge players are alert and watch carefully for partner's discards. This is the easiest way in the world to tell partner what to lead when he has a chance. When he discards low in a suit, he is discouraging you from leading that suit. A high discard when he can no longer follow suit shows that he would like you to lead that suit at your first opportunity. Sometimes you can't afford to discard a high card from your good suit. So just keep pitching low ones from the other suits and he'll get the message.

It's very important during the play of the hand that you let your partner know how many cards you have in a suit. You do this by the order in which you play them. If you play low, it shows an uneven number of cards. High shows an even number. This bit of information can help your partner count that suit and know what declarer's distribution is. The more you play the more you will realize that this is a vital part of defense, and you will automatically watch how your partner follows to a suit and be able to know exactly how many cards declarer has.

One more little tidbit while we're on the subject

of leads and signals: If the opponents bid a slam and your partner doubles it when you have the opening lead, you're a very lucky character! You don't even have to think! All you have to do is lead the suit that the dummy hand bid first. Players don't bid slams unless they expect to make them. And most certainly players don't double slams just because they hope to set them. They double for the purpose of getting the one lead that will set the hand. So when partner doubles that slam, just do as you're told and lead dummy's first bid suit. Isn't it great that there's something about opening leads that is really and truly easy!

Test Yourself

The opponent opened one no trump and his partner bid three no trump. No other bidding. What do you lead with these hands? Why?

1. ♠ Q 3
   ♥ K 8 7 5
   ♦ Q 9 4 3
   ♣ Q 10 5

   Lead the five of hearts, because it's better to lead from a king than from a queen. The king has a greater chance of survival.

2. ♠ A 7
   ♥ 10 8 5 4 2
   ♦ K Q 10
   ♣ 6 4 3

   Lead the four of hearts, because with the entries in your hand, you have a good chance of establishing your little five-card suit.

155

3. ♠ 9 6
   ♥ Q 3
   ♦ Q 6 5 4 2
   ♣ K Q 10 9

Lead the king of clubs, because it is a very strong suit and you have a good chance of taking several tricks in the suit. If you lead your four of diamonds, you may never get a diamond trick if the jack wins the first trick.

4. ♠ J 9 8 6 2
   ♥ 7
   ♦ A 4
   ♣ J 9 8 7 4

Lead the six of spades. When you have a choice between a major suit and a minor, it's better to lead the major, because the opponents would be much more apt to bid the major suit if they had it.

5. ♠ J 6 5 2
   ♥ J 10 9
   ♦ Q 3
   ♣ A J 7 6

Lead the jack of hearts. You'd rather have the club lead come up to your hand, and leading the two of spades from the jack doesn't look too promising. Just try to help your parnter.

6. You opened the bidding with one spade, but the opponents are playing the hand at three no trump, which your partner doubled. What is your lead?

   ♠ Q 10 7 5 4
   ♥ Q J 10
   ♦ 3
   ♣ A K 9 8

Lead the five of spades because your partner doubled the three no trump contract, demanding that you lead the suit you bid.

7. The opponent opened the bidding one spade, you doubled, and there were three passes. What do you lead?

♠ 8
♥ K Q 10 2
♦ A K 4 3
♣ K J 7 5

You should lead the eight of spades. Because your partner passed your take-out double, converting it into a penalty double, he has a fistful of trumps and may in time be able to lead declarer out, so he won't be able to trump your big cards.

8. You are west and the bidding was as follows. What do you lead?

♠ Q J 10 3
♥ 7 4 2
♦ 9
♣ J 7 6 5 4

NORTH	EAST	SOUTH	WEST
1 club	pass	2 hearts	pass
2 spades	pass	4 no trump	pass
5 diamonds	pass	6 hearts	pass
pass	double	pass	pass
pass			

You *must* lead a club, because your partner doubled the slam bid, demanding the lead of the first suit bid by dummy.

Your partner bid hearts and the opponents are playing four spades. What is your lead in the following hands?

9. ♠ 7 3 2
   ♥ J 10 6 4 3
   ♦ 6
   ♣ K 7 5 2

Lead the six of diamonds. You have so many hearts that your partner will probably get only one trick in the suit, and your best bet to help defeat the contract is to ruff a diamond.

10. ♠ 6 4
   ♥ K 8 3
   ♦ Q J 10 7
   ♣ 8 7 4 2

Lead the three of hearts, your partner's bid suit.

11. ♠ 8 7 5 3
   ♥ K 2
   ♦ Q J 10 7 5
   ♣ 4 2

Lead the king of hearts because your partner bid the suit, NOT because you wish to ruff. If your partner had not bid, you would have led the queen of diamonds.

11

INTRODUCING DUPLICATE

"Now that you are getting to be accomplished bridge players, it's time to try a new and exciting experience—duplicate bridge! You will be playing with your partner in a roomful of people who are all playing the same hands that you do. The object of the game is to score more points when you play the hands than the other people will.

"Duplicate bridge is not very different from the rubber bridge you have already learned; the basic game is the same. The people who run duplicate games (the directors) and also the experienced players will be glad to help you get started.

"You will enjoy it so much that you just might become permanently addicted, as have thousands of players all across the nation.

"Welcome to duplicate bridge!"

Mary Platt Vaucill

One reason bridge is such a popular game is that it's a combination of luck and skill. In rubber bridge, I'd say it's about 65 percent luck and 35 percent skill. In duplicate, lots of luck is eliminated, though certainly not all of it!

If you have played duplicate, I'm sure you've found it very stimulating and enjoyable. If you haven't played duplicate, give it a whirl and don't be discouraged by the newness of the mechanics involved.

One great plus for duplicate is that you learn so much so quickly! You can see your improvement each time you play. I really believe you learn more in ten sessions of duplicate than you'd learn in playing rubber bridge for years. You are exposed to many new systems, and you see what other players did with the same hands you held.

Let's see how this new and different form of bridge works.

You and your partner go to your local duplicate club, and perhaps there are twelve tables set up. The directors will tell you which table to go to (they are all numbered) and when you find it you will see a stack of boards in the center. These are made of aluminum or plastic, and each board has four pockets to hold the cards. There is an arrow on each board pointing north and the four compass directions are clearly marked. The boards are about ten by four inches in size and each board is numbered. One of the pockets is marked "DEALER" and the board is marked "VUL" by each pocket if that team is vulnerable for that particular hand.

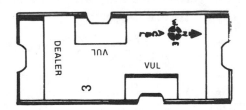

If you are a new player, the director will probably ask you and your partner to play East-West, as the North player has the responsibility for keeping the score (which is quite different from rubber bridge scoring) and it takes a little experience, though it's

160

something you will learn very quickly.

When everyone is ready to begin, the cards at each of the tables are shuffled, cut, and dealt. But instead of being dealt to each player, they are dealt into four stacks and then placed in the proper pockets. These hands stay in the same pocket all evening as each board is moved from table to table. That way every player in the room who is sitting in your position will play the same hands you do.

When the director says it's time to start, each player removes the cards from his pocket and, before he looks at his hand, he counts the cards face down to be sure there has been no misdeal or mix-up, and that all 13 cards are there. It is also good to count them after the hand has been played and before you put the cards back in the pocket.

The hand designated "dealer" starts the auction and the bidding proceeds exactly as in rubber bridge. When it is over and the opening lead has been made, the dummy hand goes down on the table. The board you are playing is left in the center of the table. The play of the hand is exactly as in rubber bridge with one very important exception. Since the hands must be kept separate to be replaced in the board after the play is completed, you may not gather up the four cards into a trick as you do in rubber bridge. Each player, when it is his turn to play, puts his card face up on the table in front of him. Another difference in the play of the hand is that declarer tells the dummy which card to play on each trick instead of reaching over and playing himself. This may be a little confusing at first, but you'll soon become accustomed to this—and even like it!

Now you may ask, "How in the world do you know who has taken which tricks? How can you tell how many tricks you have?" Very simple, really, but at first it will take a little getting used to! After each hand has played to the lead, each player places his card on that trick in front of him face *down*, and points the card in the direction of the winner. In this illustration you can see that "we" (my partner and I) have taken three tricks so far and the opponents have taken two. We proceed in this manner until all 13 cards have been played.

Let's look at a hand and see how it is bid and played. You are East and you have dealt.

```
                  NORTH
                ♠  A J 8 3
                ♥  5 2
                ♦  6 5 4 3
                ♣  A J 3

   WEST                        EAST
 ♠  K 10 9 4                 ♠  Q 7 2
 ♥  Q 7 4                    ♥  A K 9 8 6 3
 ♦  A 8 2                    ♦  K 7
 ♣  K Q 5                    ♣  4 2

                  SOUTH
                ♠  6 5
                ♥  J 10
                ♦  Q J 10 9
                ♣  10 9 8 7 6
```

Bidding:

SOUTH	WEST	NORTH	EAST
			1 heart
pass	2 no trump	pass	3 hearts
pass	4 hearts	pass	pass
pass			

You open with one heart, and your partner has a balanced hand and 14 high-card points, so he jumps to two no trump. On your minimum hand you bid three hearts and your partner bids four hearts.

South, with his miserable hand, does have a sequence, so he leads the queen of diamonds, which you take with your king. You then lead the king of hearts, followed by the ace, and the trump suit is taken care of. You then lead a small club, and dummy's king is taken by North's ace. North leads a small diamond, taken by dummy's ace. You then lead the nine of spades from dummy, North plays the jack, and your queen wins. You lead another spade, which is won by North's ace. North leads another diamond, which you trump. You cash dummy's good spade and make five hearts.

The hand might well have made the same at no trump. Who knows what the other hand would have led had West decided, with his square hand, to put the contract in no trump instead of hearts. It's certain that some pairs will, and they will probably score more points.

One thing that is very different about duplicate is that there is no part score carryover from a previous hand. Each hand is a new beginning. Honors do not count in duplicate, and the bonus points are as follows:

A game bid and made—vulnerable	500
A game bid and made—not vulnerable	300
A part score	50

With these exceptions, the scoring is exactly the same. Suppose you bid two hearts and make three. You would get 90 plus the part score bonus =140 points.

There is a traveling score slip that travels with the board, carefully folded and placed in the North pocket so that players who haven't played that board may not see what any of the other players did on that hand.

Let's look at a hand and see how it was bid at several different tables, and then look at the results of these bids on the score sheet.

NORTH
♠ A K Q 8 7
♥ K Q 7 4
♦ 5 3
♣ J 8

WEST
♠ 10 4
♥ 10 6 2
♦ K 7 6 4
♣ Q 7 6 5

EAST
♠ 9 3 2
♥ A 8 5
♦ Q 9 8 2
♣ K 3 2

SOUTH
♠ J 6 5
♥ J 9 3
♦ A J 10
♣ A 10 9 4

Bidding

NORTH	EAST	SOUTH	WEST
1 spade	pass	2 clubs	pass
2 hearts	pass	2 spades	pass
3 spades	pass	3 no trump	pass
pass	pass		

The opening lead is the two of hearts. You play low from dummy and your opponent plays the eight. You win with the nine. You play the heart jack and opponent takes his ace and leads the eight of diamonds (he does this to fool you into thinking he has no honors in his suit). You play the ten and West takes the king. The ten of hearts is led, you win in dummy, take your five spade tricks and your heart trick. Now you have left in your hand only the ace and jack of diamonds and ace of clubs. You lead a small diamond from the board and (foolishly) decide not to finesse it. So you take 10 tricks, making 430.

As you can see, you could have made five, and look at the difference in the score.

OFFICIAL A.C.B.L. TRAVELING SCORE
(Mitchell or Howell)

North player keeps score

Enter E-W Pair No.

Board No. 15

N-S Pair No.	CON-TRACT	BY	Made	Down	SCORE N-S	SCORE E-W	E-W Pair No.	Match Points
1	4 S	N	5		450		1	6½
2	5 S*	N	5		650		2	9
3	6 S	N		1		50	4	0
4	3 NT	S	4		430		6	4
5	5 S	N	5		450		8	6½
6	3 NT	S	5		460		10	8
7	3 S	N	5		200		3	1
8	3 NT	S	4		430		5	4
9	4 S	N	4		420		7	2
10	3 NT	S	4		430		9	4
11								
12								

165

You will see that duplicate scoring is very different from rubber bridge scoring, and that difference has to be understood because if affects strategy and many of the decisions you make. Each hand is a separate event. It makes no difference how many games and slams you and your partner bid during the evening, only how well you will do compared to the other pairs who hold the same cards you hold.

It's plain to see by the score that one pair who made five no trump did very well indeed, and were beaten only by the pair who wcrc lucky enough to make their five spade bid doubled by the opponents. That's one of the breaks of the game, and shows that there *is* a lot of luck involved.

Each pair will have a private score, too, on which they may record what they did on each hand after it was played. This makes it fascinating to compare the private score cards with other players at the end of the evening and see how they bid. On the other side of the private score is the convention card, on which each pair checks the conventions they use. For instance, you will show whether you use the strong two bid or the weak two bid, whether or not you open four-card majors, whether or not you play Stayman, etc., etc., etc. This is so your opponents will understand your system of bidding and may ask you about any convention they don't happen to know. Here is what it looks like:

SPECIAL DOUBLES (Describe)	DIRECT NT OVERCALLS	Names _____
Negative _____	1NT _____ to _____ HCP	General Approach _____ Pair # _____
	Jump to 2NT: ___ to ___ HCP	
Responsive _____	Unusual for Minors □	Strong Forcing Opening: 2♣ □ 2 bids □ 1♦ □ Other_____
Other _____	2 Lower Unbid □	
	Other _____	**NOTRUMP OPENING BIDS**

SIMPLE OVERCALL	Vs. Wk.□ Strong□ NT Opening	1NT _____ to _____	2NT _____ to _____ HCP
___ to ___ HCP (occ. light □)	Direct □ Balance □	1NT _____ to _____	3NT _____ to _____ HCP
Responses: New Suit Forcing □	2♣ shows ♠ ◊ ♡ ♣	2♣ Forc.□ Non-Forc.□ Stayman	Solid Suit □: _____
Cuebid Is: One-Round Force □	2◊ shows ♠ ◊ ♡ ♣	2◊ Forc.□ Non-Forc.□ Stayman	
Game Force □ Limit Raise □	2♡ shows ♠ ◊ ♡ ♣	Transfers: Jacoby□ Texas□ Other□ _____	
Other _____	2♠ shows ♠ ◊ ♡ ♣	1NT - 3♣ / 3◊ Is Invitational □	Preemptive □ Forcing □
	Other _____	Other _____	

JUMP OVERCALL	OVER OPP'S TAKEOUT DOUBLE		
	New Suit Force 1-level □ 2-level □	**MAJOR OPENINGS**	**MINOR OPENINGS**
Strong □ Interm □ Preempt □	Jp. Shift Force□ Good□ Weak□	1♡-1♠ Opening on 4 Cards	Length Promised
Special Responses _____	Redouble Implies No Fit □		4+ 3+ Shorter
	Other _____	Often Seldom Never	1♣ □ □ □
		1st-2nd □ □ □	1◊ □ □ □
OPENING PREEMPTS	Vs. Opp's Preempts Dbl. Is	3rd-4th □ □ □	
Sound Light Solid Minor	Takeout Opt. Penalty	**RESPONSES**	**RESPONSES**
3 bids □ □ □	Wk. 2's □ □ □	Double Raise Forcing □ Limit □	Double Raise
Other _____	3 Bids □ □ □	Preemptive □ Limit in Comp. □	Forcing □ Limit □ Preempt□
	Conv. takeout _____	Conv. Raise: 2NT □ 3NT □	Single Raise Forcing □
		Swiss □ Splinter □	1NT/1♦ _____ to _____ HCP
PSYCHICS Systemic □	DIRECT CUEBID	Conv. Responses: 1NT Forcing □	1◊ Resp. Conv. _____
Never Rare Occ. Frequent	Strong Takeout: Minor □ Major □	Drury □ Single Raise Constr. □	
□ □ □ □	Natural: ♣ □ ◊ □ Artif. Bids □	Other _____	Other _____
Describe: _____	Two Suits □		
Controls _____			

2♣	WK □ □ ___ to ___ HCP. Describe _____
	INT □ □ Conv. Resp. & Rebids _____
	STR □ □ 2◊ Neg. □ 2 NT Neg. □

2◊	WK □ □ ___ to ___ HCP. Describe _____
	INT □ □ Conv. Resp. & Rebids _____
	STR □ □ 2 NT Force □ 2 NT-Neg. □

SLAM CONVENTIONS		2♡	WK □ □ ___ to ___ HCP. Describe _____
Gerber _____ 4NT Var. □ _____			INT □ □ Conv. Resp. & Rebids _____
Interference over 4♣ or 4NT [Describe] _____			STR □ □ 2 NT Force □ 2 NT Neg. □

DEFENSIVE CARD PLAY		2♠	WK □ □ ___ to ___ HCP. Describe _____
Opening lead vs. SUITS: 3rd best □ 4th best □ 5th best □ Other ___			INT □ □ Conv. Resp. & Rebids _____
Mark card led: xxx AKx KQx QJx J10x 109x			STR □ □ 2 NT Force □ 2 NT Neg. □
K J10x K 109x Q 109x xxxxx			
Opening lead vs. NT: 3rd best □ 4th best □ Other _____		**OTHER CONVENTIONAL CALLS**	

(Red Dot)	Mark card led: xxx AKJx AQJx AJ109	_____
	A 1098 KQJx KQ109 KJ109 K 1098	_____
	QJ10x Q 1098 J109x 1098x xxxxx	_____

Special Carding _____ Frequent Count Signals □

If in doubt as to the meaning of a conventional call — ASK AT YOUR TURN!

Let's look at a few hands and see how we might bid them.

♠ J 4 2
♥ Q J 10 3
♦ K 7 5 2
♣ 10 9

My partner has dealt and opens one spade. The opponent passes and here is my hand. I have seven high-card points and balanced distribution, so I shall respond one no trump. Now the left hand opponent bids two hearts and my partner passes. You know, a pass is a *very* descriptive call at the bridge table. My partner is telling me loud and clear that he had a minimum opening bid.

Here is partner's hand:

♠ K Q 10 8 5
♥ 6 4
♦ A J 9
♣ K 4 3

My right hand opponent passes and it's my turn again. I'm not ready to give up yet. I have three cards including the jack in my partner's suit and a doubleton. I could have raised him instead of bidding one no trump, so I shall raise him to two spades now. If the opponent bids three hearts, I just might be able to give him a lot of grief, and I don't think we're in any jeopardy at two spades. Never forget that in duplicate it is vitally important to fight for the little under-game hands!

Here's a hand that gives us reason to think hard! My partner has opened the bidding one no trump, which is always a happy thing. The opponent bids two hearts and here I sit looking at this:

♠ 10 6
♥ Q 6 3
♦ 8 5
♣ A J 10 9 7 6

My partner has at least 16 points. I don't know where they are, but maybe there is an honor in the club suit. So we *could* have six very healthy tricks here. I have the queen of hearts over the opponent's bid, which is a very comforting thing—and we have a minimum of 23 high-card points (a far cry from the 26 we count on to produce game), but the six-card suit tempts me to take a slight risk and bid three no trump. Why not? In duplicate you can't afford to bid and play timidly. Make yourself into an aggressive bidder and an optimistic player if that is not your natural tendancy. It isn't always easy to decide when to make the risky bid or the risky play, but remember that you won't be a consistent winner if you always take the "safe" course.

One of the tough things in any bridge game, rubber or duplicate, is to decide whether or not to bid a slam or be cautious and settle for less when you have an exciting hand. Here's one that's questionable. Your partner dealt. Here is his hand:

♠ A K 5 2
♥ 7 6
♦ K 10 8 3
♣ Q J 7

He opens one diamond. The opponents pass throughout the bidding.

Your hand:

♠ 3
♥ K Q 10 5
♦ A Q J 7 4
♣ A 6 3

Your hand qualifies beautifully for a jump shift in support of diamonds, so you bid two hearts. Partner's next bid is two spades. You have already told him about your enormous hand, so now you will tell him about your beautiful diamond fit by bidding three diamonds.

Partner has nothing more to say, so he makes that clear by bidding three no trump. You aren't willing to settle for a mere game without further investigation, so you decide to cue bid your ace of clubs (remember the lesson on showing controls?). After your four club bid, partner bids four spades. So you now know that he has the ace of spades but not the ace of hearts, since he would have bid that if he did have it. Here comes the moment of truth. Should you take a flier on six diamonds or not? If your partner's strength is additional high cards in the spade suit (which was his rebid after your jump shift), they will be wasted values. So you decide that the best and safest contract would be to give up on the slam and play the hand at no trump. You bid four no trump, knowing that your partner will pass as he could not possibly confuse your bid with the Blackwood four no trump. Why? Because you have been showing controls after you set the suit. So he realizes that in your judgment you'll get a better score playing the hand at no trump than at diamonds.

The evening of your first venture in duplicate bridge goes on with never a dull moment. As East-West, you and your partner move from table to table in ascending order, (i.e., from table five to six, from six to seven, etc.), as the boards you play move in the opposite direction (from five to four and four to three), so you will never see those hands you've played again. North-South remain in the same seats all night. When the game is over, you will probably stay around to see how well you did. You may watch the director as he matches points with the scores, or you may be busy comparing your private score with other people's scores.

The match point method of scoring is very simple really. Each hand counts equally toward your final score. You may get lots of match points on a board when you were set a trick or two. It is strictly a process of *comparing* what you did on the hand with what other players in your seat did. With twelve tables in play, the top number of match points on each board will be 11 and the bottom will be zero. In other words, the pair who scores best will be awarded 11, second best will get 10, and on down the line. The director awards the North-South pairs match points first. After that he gives match points to the East-West pairs. If a North-South pair gets top on a board (in this case 11) the East-West pair that played against them on that board would get 0. If the North-South pair gets seven, their East-West opponents would score four. If the North-South pair wins one match point, the East-West pair would be awarded 10. If more than one pair score the same on the board, the director averages the successive points (i.e.: if three pairs come in second, the director adds 10 + 9 + 8 = 27; this he divides by three, awarding each pair nine match points).

If 24 boards were played during the session (two boards at each table) the *average* score each pair could make would be 132 match points (24 x 5 1/2). You always hope very much to be average or better, and *you'll find that the pairs who get better-than-average scores on all the boards are the ones who usually win.* It's great to get a top board and sad when you get a bottom, but playing good, steady bridge is what pays off! In other words, a 60-65 percent game has a mighty good chance of coming out ahead of the pack!

When the game is over and the scores are figured, for goodness' sake don't be discouraged if you didn't do too well! It has been a brand new experience for you, and it takes a little getting used to. Next time you play, it won't seem so unnatural to keep the cards in front of you, and when you are declarer to ask the dummy to play each of his cards instead of reaching over and playing them yourself.

Contract bridge is contract bridge, but you will find many differences in your approach to duplicate and your approach to rubber bridge. You have always been aware of the importance of vulnerability—both your own and your opponents'—in rubber bridge, but in duplicate this factor is even more vital in making decisions about how much to bid, whether or not to sacrifice, whether or not to double.

I've heard it said that duplicate does away with the element of luck. Not so! It most certainly minimizes it, but I do feel that it's tough luck if I have to play a very difficult hand against the strongest pair in the room, and their defense is superb. They manage to set me, and against weaker opponents I could have made the contract! On the

172

other hand, I consider myself extremely lucky when the opening leader fails to make that killer lead which could have ruined me! So, we'll roll with the punches, take our good boards and our bad ones, and learn more and more about this new and exciting game of duplicate. Most important of all—ENJOY!

Test Yourself

(These are normal hands that you would bid about the same in duplicate as you would in rubber bridge, so this is a review to emphasize important points we have covered.)

The opponent has opened the bidding one diamond. There are two passes. What will you do with the following hands?

1. ♠ K J 10 6
   ♥ A Q 5
   ♦ 6 2
   ♣ 9 6 5 4

   You will double. The balancing double shows about 10 points, which is what you have, and you would never consider passing and letting the opponents steal this hand with a one diamond bid.

2. ♠ Q J 8 7 6
   ♥ A 3
   ♦ 5 2
   ♣ 9 6 5 4

   Bid one spade. The hand is too weak to double but you aren't willing to sell out for one diamond.

3. ♠ A 9
   ♥ 4 3
   ♦ Q J 10 6 2
   ♣ 9 6 5 4

Pass. It's too bad the bid is only one diamond, but you will take a lot of tricks—and you don't have the ammu—nition to try to push them up higher. So just do the best you can to set the bid.

The opponent opens one diamond. You pass and opener's partner passes. What do you do with the following hands when your partner reopens with one heart or a double?

4. ♠ K 9 2
   ♥ A 10 6 3
   ♦ 8 5
   ♣ A 7 6 4

If partner reopens with one heart, you will pass, as there is no chance of a game. If he reopens with a double, you will, of course, bid one heart.

5. ♠ K 9 2
   ♥ A 10 9
   ♦ Q 10 9 7
   ♣ A 5 3

Pass if your partner bids one heart. You have 14 points, but the chance of a game is pretty slim. If you'd prefer, you could bid one no trump. If your partner reopens with a double and your oponents are vulnerable, you could pass for penalties. Otherwise you would bid two no trump.

The opponent opens one diamond. You pass, opener's partner bids two diamonds, and there are two passes. It's your turn, so what will you do with the following?

6. ♠ Q J 7
   ♥ K J 10 5
   ♦ 6 4 3
   ♣ 7 5 3

What a miserable situation! But something is wrong somewhere. So just bite the bullet and bid two hearts. You probably won't get doubled and your partner surely has some values.

7. ♠ Q J 7
   ♥ K J 10 5
   ♦ 6 4 3
   ♣ A 7 5

This hand is an ace better than the last one, so now, with your eleven points, you may double—and hope not to get in trouble.

There have been two passes. In third position, what is your action with the following?

8. ♠ 7 6 5
   ♥ K Q J 5 2
   ♦ 7 6
   ♣ K 4 3

Bid one heart. You'd like to have more than nine high-card points, but your suit is good, and if the opponents get the final contract, you'd like to have your partner lead a heart.

9. ♠ K Q J 5 2
   ♥ 10 9 7
   ♦ 7 6
   ♣ 5 4 3

Pass. It does not pay to open a hand with six high-card points in *any* circumstance.

175

10. ♠ K 9 8 5 3
    ♥ K Q J
    ♦ 7 6
    ♣ 5 4 3

Pass. You have nine high-card points, but your suit is very poor. Don't be tempted to bid this one.

11. ♠ K 9 8 5 3
    ♥ K Q J
    ♦ 7 6
    ♣ Q 5 4

Bid one spade. Even with a poor suit you will almost always open the bidding in third position with 11 high-card points.

12
DUPLICATE STRATEGY

"To be sure, there are some very interesting differences between duplicate and rubber bridge strategies. In duplicate, you never start bidding a hand with either side having a part score, as each hand is a new beginning. Being aware of which side is vulnerable and which side is not may be even more important in duplicate than in rubber bridge. Being aware of what other players are likely to do when they get the same cards (and what other opponents may do) is probably the most crucial difference of all—and that means imagining how your score will compare with the scores of the other players. Once you have learned that, you will have learned one of the real secrets to success in duplicate bridge. Good luck to you!"

Thomas K. Sanders
Carol Sanders

There are a few simple things that should be topmost in your mind when you first begin to try your luck at duplicate bridge. Let's list them just to get our thinking organized, and then we'll discuss them.

1. Remember that you are competing with all the other players in the room who are sitting in your same position. They are your *real* opponents—the ones you are trying to "outthink" and "outsmart."

2. In duplicate, minor suits are even less desirable than they are in rubber bridge. If possible, try to find a final contract in no trump or a major suit.
3. Remember to notice carefully the vulnerability on each hand—both your opponents' and your own—as this will make a big difference in your bidding.
4. Part scores are vitally important, and you should fight valiantly for them (but not foolishly!).
5. In duplicate, it is even more important to balance in fourth position than it is in rubber bridge. Don't ever be willing to sell out cheaply!
6. You should be especially aware of the value of opening with fewer than 13 points in third position. In fourth position, you should not be quite so eager.
7. Always be aware of the importance of ethical behavior, i.e., don't bid or pass quickly; don't bid or pass too slowly; don't change the tone of your voice or your expression.

Let's look at two hands and see how the bidding goes. This is the opening hand:

♠ A 10 7 6
♥ A K J 4 3
♦ J 9 8
♣ 3

Here is the partner's hand:

♠ K Q 8 3
♥ Q 6 2
♦ A 6 3
♣ 8 7 4

Bidding:

OPENER	OPPONENT	PARTNER	OPPONENT
1 heart	pass	1 spade	pass
2 spades	pass	3 hearts	pass
4 spades	pass	pass	pass

The opening bidder feels his team has a game in either hearts or spades but he is well aware that the other players who will have these hands will reach a game contract, too. Making an extra trick is vitally important, and it is usually advantageous to play a trump suit in which the cards are four/four rather than five/three. He very wisely chooses to play the spade suit, and sure enough, they make an extra trick that they wouldn't have made if hearts had been trumps. I don't know why it is that so many people would rather play a five-card trump suit. In rubber bridge it isn't vital to make those extra tricks, but in duplicate all the other players who are sitting in your position are your "unseen" opponents and they will be trying hard to do a little better than you do on each and every hand.

Even in rubber bridge, we avoid game contracts in minor suits when possible because it's so hard to take eleven tricks. But in duplicate there's another much more compelling reason for trying to avoid them. Let's suppose there's no problem taking eleven tricks in the combined hands. We are not vulnerable, so the bonus for making a game is 300 points.

Five clubs	= 100 + 300 = 400 total
Five spades	= 150 + 300 = 450 total
Five no trump	= 160 + 300 = 460 total

So, the pair that bids the hands shown below at a game in no trump is the clear winner!

OPENER	PARTNER
♠ K Q 9 2	♠ A 10 7 3
♥ 10 2	♥ K 4
♦ A 8	♦ J 6 4
♣ A Q J 6 4	♣ K 10 3 2

Bidding:

OPENER	OPPONENT	PARTNER	OPPONENT
1 club	1 heart	1 spade	pass
2 spades	pass	2 no trump	pass
3 no trump	pass	pass	pass

The question of who is vulnerable and who isn't is of the utmost importance in duplicate. It can help you make the choice between setting the opponents or trying to score yourself. It will help you decide whether or not a sacrifice bid would be desirable.

Let's look at a hand and make decisions. Remember, the bonus for a vulnerable game is 500. When not vulnerable, it is 300.

In this illustration, partner has opened one no trump and the opponent overcalls two hearts.

♠ K Q 9 7
♥ K J 6
♦ A 2
♣ 8 7 5 3

With this nice 13-count hand of mine opposite partner's no trump, it certainly looks like we should make four no trump, doesn't it? If we are vulnerable, we'd get 630 points—not vulnerable would be 430. I fully expect to set their two-heart bid by two tricks. If they aren't vulnerable, we'd get 300 points, so that would be no good! If they are vulnerable, our score would be 500. If we are vulnerable, our 630 game would be much better than setting them. But if the opponents are vulnerable and we are not, I shall double them and get 500 instead of 430 for our non-vulnerable game. You can see that it takes a little thinking and figuring to come up with the best decision for the various circumstances, doesn't it? But you'll get used to it. And it's quite simple, really.

When you realize that only one out of every three hands played at the bridge table contains a game, you will see how very important the part scores are. They are well worth fighting for in this competitive game.

Always remember that when the opponents stop bidding at a low part score, you should leap into the fray even with a rather poor hand. The cards are *somewhere*, and since the opponents aren't loaded, your partner must have some values, too. So, in effect, you are bidding on your partner's cards. By the same token, if your partner is the one who suddenly comes to life after silence, for heaven's sake, don't get excited. Don't count on him for much, as he is expecting some strength in your hand and he'll surely need it!

Let's look at some hands. The opponent has opened one diamond and there are two passes. It's up to you. What would you do with these hands?

♠ K 9 4 3 2
♥ A 4 2
♦ 9
♣ 10 5 4 2

This hand is too weak even for a balancing double, but you mustn't let them play one diamond. So, knowing that your partner won't take you too seriously, you should bid one spade.

♠ K 6 4 2
♥ K Q 10 8 6
♦ 4
♣ 10 9 7

You should overcall one heart because you have a good five-card suit.

♠ K Q 5 4
♥ 7 6 5 2
♦ 6 3
♣ A Q 8

With this hand you would reopen the bidding by doubling. You have as good a chance at a part score as the opponents have.

In the back of our minds there always lurks the thought of a part score possibility, and whenever we can take action that will perhaps put us on the track, we should do so. In this case, you are in second position. Your opponent has opened with one diamond. What should you do with these hands?

♠ 9 6 4
♥ K Q J 8 6
♦ 4
♣ K 9 7 3

You have a good suit and the hand has good distribution, so you should bid a heart. When you have anything as

182

positive as this to offer, you should do it, and perhaps take pressure off your partner.

♠ K 8 6
♥ K 10 6 3 2
♦ 3
♣ K 4 3 2

You should pass this hand because the suit is so poor, but you have enough strength to be a big help to your partner, who will not let the opponents buy a cheap bid. You can raise anything or bid hearts if he doubles.

In rubber bridge we certainly recommend opening hands in third position that we would have passed as dealer or second hand. In duplicate, it is even more important to avail yourself of this opportunity, but if you have a bad hand you need to have a good suit.

With this hand, I would most certainly open third hand:

♠ K Q J 7 2
♥ K 10 6
♦ 9 4
♣ 7 5 3

I have a good spade suit, and how do my opponents know whether I'm strong or weak? They don't have X-ray eyes! I'd even open one spade without the jack of spades.

Here's another one to think about:

♠ K Q J 5　　　I wouldn't hesitate a minute
♥ Q J 9 8　　　to open this 10 high-card
♦ 6 2　　　　　point hand in third position.
♣ J 8 6　　　　My bid? Well, I have a
　　　　　　　　choice, but I'm sure no one
　　　　　　　　would make the mistake of
　　　　　　　　opening one club! The
　　　　　　　　choice between spades and
　　　　　　　　hearts should be an easy one,
　　　　　　　　too. Let's open this hand one
　　　　　　　　heart, so we won't take a
　　　　　　　　chance on not finding a pos-
　　　　　　　　sible heart fit. If partner has
　　　　　　　　spades he'll bid them, where
　　　　　　　　if I bid spades and he happens
　　　　　　　　to have hearts, he probably
　　　　　　　　couldn't go to the two level.

Fourth hand opens are a little more iffy! Some
duplicate players never pass in fourth position, no
matter how scratchy the hand happens to be. I feel
they are usually digging their own graves, and in
most cases would do well to throw the hand in. However, with 11 or more points in high cards—open!
With ten points in high cards and a good spade suit,
I'd open, especially if I had some good length in the
heart suit. Here's a hand that I think is well worth
a fourth hand open. I'd probably open with a heart
if the major suits were reversed.

♠ A Q J 10 7
♥ 10 9 8 4
♦ K 3 2
♣ 5

We need not go into great detail on the subject of manners at a duplicate game because I'm sure that you would never dream of divulging anything about your hand by word or gesture in a rubber bridge game; but I'd just like to point out that it is even more important to be careful when playing duplicate. Remember all of those other people in the room who will play the same cards. You wouldn't want anyone to have even a very slight advantage!

Test Yourself

You are vulnerable. What is your response to partner's opening three club bid and why?

1. ♠ K 10 7 ♥ A 6 4 ♦ Q J 10 7 ♣ Q 6 3		Bid three no trump. You have stops in the other three suits. With three clubs in your hand, you'll have no trouble setting up the long suit.
2. ♠ A 6 ♥ VOID ♦ K Q J 9 7 3 2 ♣ A 10 4 2		Six clubs—hoping they won't lead a spade.
3. ♠ A J 7 ♥ K 3 2 ♦ Q 9 8 7 2 ♣ 7 6		Pass and hope the opponents can't bid.

There have been two passes. What should you do?

4. ♠ 9 8 7 6 Pass. If your good suit were
   ♥ K Q 10 8 4 spades, you'd open.
   ♦ K 9
   ♣ 5 3

5. ♠ 8 4 2 Pass—not strong enough
   ♥ A J 9 7 5 even in third position.
   ♦ K 10 3
   ♣ 4 3

6. ♠ K Q 7 6 4 A good question. If you open
   ♥ 8 one spade, you will cross
   ♦ K J 6 3 your fingers and hope *not* to
   ♣ 8 3 2 hear two hearts from partner. You *want* to pass anything he bids, but you
   couldn't pass two hearts. So,
   you would have to rebid two
   spades. Maybe you'd be better off passing to begin with!

There have been three passes. What should you do
and why with the following hands?

7. ♠ 8 You would pass because
   ♥ A J 10 7 6 there is too big a chance that
   ♦ 7 3 the opponents will get a part
   ♣ K J 6 5 2 score in spades.

8. ♠ A Q 10 5 2
   ♥ 10 7 3 2
   ♦ K J 8
   ♣ 2

You would open this hand one spade because it's a pretty good suit and you also have four hearts.

9. ♠ Q 6 4
   ♥ K 7
   ♦ Q J 10 9 6
   ♣ K 10 5

You would pass this hand in spite of 11 high-card points. It has no aces and is very scratchy.

10. ♠ K Q 10 7 6 5
    ♥ 4 2
    ♦ 8 4 3
    ♣ K 5

You would open this hand two spades *if* you were playing weak two bids. Otherwise, you'd pass.

13
DUPLICATE TOURNAMENTS AND TRICKS

"Just about everyone who enjoys playing bridge at the local duplicate club, sooner or later ends up going to the larger tournaments. A tournament is a giant duplicate game with hundreds of people playing bridge at the same time. Tournaments last for a full weekend, or even for a week or more. Each day a new event is held, so that you may enter a tournament for only a day or an evening.

"Experts and beginners alike have found that a tournament is fun and is an exciting challenge. I hope to welcome you to one soon!"

Mary Platt Vencill

Most bridge players, after they have played some duplicate and become comfortable with the mechanics of the game, will get the urge to go further afield than the local club and try their luck and their new-found skills at a tournament. We're going to talk about tournaments and tricks—the tricks we try to take and the tricks we occasionally use to try to deceive our worthy opponents.

There are three kinds of tournaments:

1. Sectionals—here you'll see 200 or 300 people at a time playing bridge. They usually last three days—Friday, Saturday, and Sunday.

2. Regionals—three or four times as many people compete here and they usually last five or six days.
3. Nationals—which are even larger and last for eight to nine days.

Bridge tournaments are open to anyone who wants to come and play. You may even go just to watch if you are careful not to talk and disrupt the players. Usually there is a new event every day which you may enter simply by paying a fee, which is less than the price of the average movie. You may play in a one-session event (afternoon only or evening only) or in a championship event (two sessions). But you don't have to be a champion to enter!

Tournaments are exciting! Many people are there, all for the same purpose—to win master points. Master points are the bonus points you get for winning or coming in second or third at a tournament or in a local game. In every event at a tournament, about one-third of the players win at least some master points.

If you join the American Contract Bridge League (ACBL), which is the national organization for duplicate bridge players, all of the match points you win will be added up in their computer, and you will gain in rank as you improve and play more duplicate. When you get one master point, you become a Junior Master, 20 points makes you a Master, 100 points a Senior Master, 200 points an Advanced Senior Master, and 300 points (some of them won in major tournaments) a Life Master, which is the highest ACBL ranking. By the way, if you join the ACBL you will automatically receive the monthly magazine which shows the schedule for upcoming tournaments and also includes articles about bidding and play strategy.

190

To join send $12.00 for a one year membership to:

The American Contract Bridge League (ACBL)
P.O. Box 161192
Memphis, TN 38186
(901) 332-5586

There is a coupon in the back of this book for the ACBL membership.

It's worth emphasizing that at tournaments anyone may enter. Some events arc cvcn rcstrictcd so that only inexperienced players (those with fewer than 20 master points) may enter. So you needn't worry about competing with international champions—though you may if you want the extra challenge!

If you arrive at a tournament without a partner, you will find a partnership desk where someone is assigned to match you up with another person who doesn't have a partner. They always try to match up two people who havc about thc samc amount of experience.

Each event is divided into sections, with no more than about 16 tables per section. You may win or come in second or third or fourth in your section without worrying about what people in the rest of the room are doing.

The people who run tournaments (and also local club games) are called directors. The director's most important job is to help all players and make sure that everyone enjoys the game. Other important jobs are to make sure that the contest is as fair as it can be and to calculate the final scores and determine the winners.

You will notice directors:

1. before the game, selling entries and making sure that everyone gets to his or her assigned place;
2. during the game, when players call them to the table to settle any irregularity that occurs during the play of a hand (we will talk more about that later); and
3. after the game, scoring and posting the final results.

Directors are *always* available to answer players' questions. You will find them especially helpful if you explain that you are a new tournament bridge player. If a new player isn't treated as a guest of honor, someone is doing something wrong!

Now, I said I would talk more about what happens when a director is called to the table during the bidding or play of a hand. This happens very often, and you certainly shouldn't be disturbed or alarmed when it happens at your table. These are a few of the most frequent circumstances when a director should be called:

- the wrong person leads to a trick;
- someone bids or passes when it's not his turn;
- someone revokes (fails to follow suit when he could have done so);
- one or more hands contain a number of cards other than 13, such as when a card is lost or ends up in the wrong hand;
- a card is exposed prematurely, either during the bidding or during the play, except for declarer's and dummy's card; and
- there is a possibility that someone at the table might have received unauthorized information, which means information other than that which is conveyed by a bid or the play of a card.

For each of these situations and dozens of others,

there is a set procedure for straightening things out; and it is the director's responsibility to take care of it. When the director is called to the table, he or she will first find out what has happened and then explain what should be done next. If you don't understand what to do, you should be sure to ask. If you don't understand why things were done as they were, ask the director for a complete explanation after the session is over.

All of the situations I've listed are infractions of the laws of contract bridge, but they are also mistakes that *anyone* is likely to make. For each infraction, there is a specific penalty, and, of course, players should accept the prescribed penalty in good grace. Then the game will proceed as though nothing had happened. It's a mighty good idea to get to know the laws of contract bridge (for a summary of these laws, see the next chapter).

A director may also come to the table if the play is too slow. Tournament bridge is a timed event, with about seven minutes allowed for each hand. You can imagine the chaos in a room with hundred of players if everyone played at a different speed! So the directors will make sure that play proceeds on schedule—which is necessary to maintain order and fair to all players.

Finally, a director should be called to the table if anyone does or says anything discourteous. This happens *very* seldom, but unfortunately, in the heat of competition, some players violate the proprieties—an important part of the laws. If this should happen at your table, keep calm, call the director, and trust the offending behavior will be stopped and/or penalized.

Now, we'll look at a simple example of a hand where you would need to understand how the laws work.

NORTH
♠ K 7 6 4
♥ 10 8 6
♦ A Q 7 5 2
♣ 6

WEST
♠ J 5 3
♥ J 5 4 3
♦ 10 8
♣ K 8 7 2

EAST
♠ 2
♥ A 9 2
♦ K J 9 4
♣ A J 10 9 4

SOUTH
♠ A Q 10 9 8
♥ K Q 7
♦ 6 3
♣ Q 5 3

Bidding:

NORTH	EAST	SOUTH	WEST
	1 club	1 spade	2 clubs
3 spades	pass	4 spades	pass
pass	pass		

West leads the two of clubs and his partner takes the trick with the ace. When East leads back the two of spades, the four of diamonds accidentally falls out of his hand and onto the table face up. The director should be called! The four of diamonds has been exposed prematurely and is a penalty card. A penalty card must be played at the first legal opportunity.

South knows this, of course, and quite properly takes advantage of the situation by taking the spade in his hand and leading a diamond at the *very* next trick. He *knows* East must play the four of diamonds, so he wins a cheap trick in the dummy hand; otherwise he would have lost the diamond finesse. Now South, by playing carefully, will lose only one more trick (the ace of hearts) and will make five spades on a hand where everyone else is making only four. In a tournament, this seemingly meaningless overtrick can make a huge difference in your score, and you should not feel that it's unfair to take advantage of your opponent's mistake. It would be unfair *not* to (unfair to all the other East-West pairs who did not make this error).

We'll look at another hand where the director was called. We won't need the East-West hands to illustrate this one.

NORTH
♠ A Q 9 7 5
♥ A 2
♦ 9 8
♣ A 8 6 3

SOUTH
♠ 6 3
♥ 7
♦ A K 7 2
♣ K Q J 10 7 5

Bidding:

NORTH	EAST	SOUTH	WEST
1 spade	2 hearts	2 clubs	

The director was called immediately—South must have been star-gazing or something, not to have bid three clubs over his opponent's two hearts! The director gave the ruling: If South made his insufficient bid just barely sufficient and in the same suit (i.e.: three clubs), then there would be no penalty. So the bidding proceeded, they got to their slam, and all was well! A much happier ending than the last sad story.

Now let's talk about bidding some hands. We have talked so much about vulnerability that I'm beginning to sound like a broken record, but it is so *very* important that I stress it on every occasion. Here is a hand where we are *not* vulnerable and the opponents are.

♠ K 10 8 6 4 3 2
♥ 6
♦ K J 2
♣ 9 5

I'll open this hand three spades, because if the opponents can bid and make a vulnerable game at hearts they will get 620 points—so it is to my advantage to be set a mere 500. It's important to remember that there is almost no such thing as bidding a preempt when *you* are vulnerable and the opponents *aren't*, but almost any seven-card suit should preempt when *they* are vulnerable and *you* are not!

One very valuable little tip to remember: When

196

you are in first or second position (in other words, before your partner has had a chance to bid), you should hesitate to open a hand with three diamonds or three clubs if you have as many as four cards in either major suit. Let's look at a hand and see why.

DEALER
♠ 9 8 6 2
♥ 3
♦ A K Q 7 6 4 2
♣ 10

PARTNER
♠ A K 10 7 3
♥ A 4 2
♦ 9 3
♣ Q 8 7

If the dealer opens this hand three diamonds, the partnership will miss a beautiful game in spades—so, in first or second position think twice before you make a minor suit preempt if you have anything in either major suit. It would be a pity to shut out your partner when the purpose of the bid is to shut out the opponents!

Let's look at a hand that was played in a tournament many years ago which is very interesting when we think of all the various possibilities. North-South are vulnerable, and East-West are not vulnerable. North is the dealer.

NORTH
- ♠ 7
- ♥ A K 6 4
- ♦ 9 8 5
- ♣ A K J 7 3

WEST
- ♠ 5
- ♥ 10 8 7 2
- ♦ K Q J 3
- ♣ Q 8 4 2

EAST
- ♠ Q J 10 9 8 3 2
- ♥ 5
- ♦ 10 7 4
- ♣ 9 6

SOUTH
- ♠ A K 6 4
- ♥ Q J 9 3
- ♦ A 6 2
- ♣ 10 5

Bidding:

NORTH	EAST	SOUTH	WEST
1 club	3 spades	3 no trump	pass
pass	pass		

You will notice that the preemptive overcall by non-vulnerable East kept the North-South hands from ever bidding their hearts, and four hearts was obviously the better contract. The South hand made his three no trump bid for 600 points while the other teams scored 620 for the four hearts. In a case like this, when South realized he would be very low on this board anyway, he should have decided to "go for broke" and try the club finesse. If it loses he's going down—but it makes so *little* difference in tournament bridge if your bottom boards are rock bottom or just a little bottom. You will get a big, fat zero on

198

the board anyway, so why not take a chance and perhaps get a *top!* This he would surely have done if he had made six no trump instead of just the three no trump which he bid!

Here's another hand that was actually played in a recent tournament. This time East-West are vulnerable and North-South are not. As we have seen, being not vulnerable is often a license to steal, or at least a time when you can afford to be slightly risky and frisky in your bidding.

NORTH
♠ K 10 9 8 6 4
♥ Q 9 6 5
♦ A 3
♣ 7

WEST
♠ A 3
♥ A J 4
♦ K J 8 7 2
♣ A 9 5

EAST
♠ Q
♥ 7 3 2
♦ Q 10 9 6 4
♣ K Q J 4

SOUTH
♠ J 7 5 2
♥ K 10 8
♦ 5
♣ 10 8 6 3 2

Bidding:

NORTH	EAST	SOUTH	WEST
			1 no trump
2 hearts	3 diamonds	3 spades	3 no trump
4 spades	4 no trump	5 spades	double
pass	pass	pass	

199

North decided to overcall the West one no trump bid with two hearts (a conventional bid which shows heart and spade distribution—usually five of each). East bid three diamonds and South, knowing his partner was using the convention, bid three spades. North might easily have passed the three no trump bid, but he realized that with East's three diamond bid the opponents would probably make an easy three no trump and, not being vulnerable, decided he could afford to go set three tricks doubled for a loss of 500 against the 600 the opponents make at no trump. So he bid four spades. East hated to be conned out of a game, so he bid four no trump. Now South was stubborn too, and bid five spades! Of course, this was doubled—and can you imagine how happy South was to see the dummy hand go down on the table! This turned out to be a very profitable venture for North-South. The hand played like a dream and they were set only one trick.

All of this just goes to show that there is never a dull moment in tournament bridge! The wildest things can happen and do!

There is a great deal more doubling for penalties in tournament bridge than in rubber bridge, because this is a game of percentages—and the low scores you get when the opponents manage to make a doubled contract are offset by the high scores you get when you set them for more points than you would have made with a part-score or a game. There is an old saying in duplicate, "If all of your doubles work, you probably aren't doubling enough!"

Some people feel that players who use the weak no trump have an advantage when it comes to doubling part-score bids. Opponents may be more careful about overcalling a strong no trump. Here is an example—this hand opens one no trump (weak):

♠ K 10 8 4
♥ J 6 3
♦ J 4
♣ A K 9 6

Here is partner's hand:

♠ J 3
♥ Q 10 5 2
♦ A K 9 6
♣ 8 7 5

With 10 high-card points he knows that he and his partner have the majority of the points so he will double any overcall the opponent makes. You may be unlucky. The overcall may be on a freak hand. But more often than not (about three times out of four) you will pick up a lot of points when the most your side could have hoped for was a little part-score. So, don't fret about the times where opponents make the bid. If you think you have a good shot at setting them—double!

You remember, we have said in the past that partner should not raise a preemptive bid unless he has sufficient values for game. In tournaments your thinking will be a little different.

Here's my partner's opening hand:

♠ 7
♥ K Q J 9 6 5 4
♦ Q 7 6
♣ 10 9

We are *not* vulnerable. He opens three hearts and the opponent passes.

Here is my hand:

♠ 8 2
♥ A 10 7 2
♦ 10 9 5 2
♣ 8 6 2

I'm surprised the opponent passed when I have nothing but the ace of hearts. That means the other opponent has everything in the deck, and the three heart bid won't stop him for a minute. So I shall quickly bid four hearts—maybe even five! All I can do is to try to make my partner's preempt even more preemptive.

One sometimes has the idea that tournament players make lots of psychic, or deceptive, bids. Very few players make these bids on weak hands. They are usually made on a good hand for the purpose of trying to fool their opponents into making a lead that will help them. Remember, in tournaments, we're always trying to eke out that important over-trick.

Here's a hand that will illustrate a bit of deception. Your partner has opened one spade.

♠ 8 6
♥ K J 10 5
♦ A 6 3
♣ K Q 10 8

You are almost sure the final contract will be three no trump, unless your partner bids hearts next time. Your normal bid would be a jump to two no trump, wouldn't it? But, right now might be a good time to make a deceptive bid—to try to keep the opponents from making their best lead against a no trump. You'd be delighted with either a heart or club lead, wouldn't you? So instead of bidding two no trump, you will bid two diamonds! The bidding goes on and after your partner's two spade rebid, you jump to three no trump.

Here is partner's hand:

♠ A Q J 7 3
♥ Q 6 2
♦ J 7 4
♣ A 9

So you see that the combined hands will do *much* better if they do not get an opening diamond lead. Pretty neat trick, isn't it?

This next hand is not really deceptive, but just a matter of arithmatic—and using your head. You would do this in a tournament, but would not be

203

nearly so apt to in rubber bridge. You are *not* vulnerable and the opponents are vulnerable.

Here is your hand:

♠ 4 2
♥ 7 5
♦ Q J 10 9 7 6 5 3
♣ 6

Bidding:

PARTNER	OPPONENT	YOU	OPPONENT
			2 spades
pass	3 spades	pass	4 no trump
pass	5 diamonds	pass	6 spades
pass	pass	?	

Now is the time to do some serious thinking and figuring. There they are at six spades after their opening strong two bid! They must be missing one ace—or they'd have bid seven. So, you can count on your partner having an ace. Making six spades would give them 1430 points and your prospects of setting them look nil. But, at diamonds you would go down only six tricks—and not vulnerable, they would score only 1100 points! A major victory for your side! So, you bid seven diamonds—and your opponents can only gnash their teeth!

One very important thing about playing in tournaments is the decisions you make about when to double the opponents for a sure set, and when to bid one more yourself.

Here is a hand where that decision must be made. You are vulnerable. The opponents are not.

♠ A Q J 9 8
♥ A Q 7 3
♦ 6 5
♣ A 8

Bidding:

YOU	OPPONENT	PARTNER	OPPONENT
1 spade	pass	4 spades	5 diamonds
?			

Now, what do you do? In rubber bridge you'd probably just double and get your sure profit. But in a tournament, this might not be enough. You can't take a chance on just getting 500 points for setting them, when you're sure you could make 620 in a game at spades. So, you really have no choice. You must bid five spades and try like mad to make it.

We'll look at one more hand where a little deception might pay off:

♠ K 7 3
♥ Q J 7 4
♦ K 9 8
♣ J 10 9

Bidding:

PARTNER	OPPONENT	ME	OPPONENT
1 spade	pass	2 spades	pass
pass			

When my partner passes my two spades, I know his hand is minimum. The opponent knows it too, and can't possibly resist balancing. After all, I sound very weak with my raise to two spades. So, he bids and, of course, it must be at the three level. So, no matter what he bids, I shall double him!

My partner's hand might look like this:

♠ A 10 9 8 4   A *real* minimum, with very
♥ 6   little trick taking value ex-
♦ Q J 7 6 3   cept as declarer. So, he will
♣ K 8   bid three spades.

But his hand might look like this:

♠ A 10 9 8 4   A very different situation.
♥ 6 3   This hand is great for de-
♦ A J 4   fense. So he passes.
♣ K Q 6

It is also possible to be fooled by the opponent's opening bid. Sometimes, for instance, when leading from a king, he might lead a rather high card—10 or nine—to make you think he's short suited perhaps. Tricky leads can cause declarer a lot of grief. However, it isn't wise to overdo these little ruses we use. Nothing is effective if used too much, so, let's pick our times for tricky business pretty carefully.

If you haven't yet played in a tournament, I do

hope you will soon. It's exciting and full of suspense, and you'll find yourself caught up in the spirit of competition. You could play against other people with limited tournament experience, or, if you wish, you could play against some of the finest players in the world. What a thrill! There are many games under way at the same time. The larger the tournament, the more games. In a way, tournaments may be compared to track and field meets—any number of events going on simultaneously. Some are short, lasting only one session. Others are longer and may take three or more days with sessions afternoons and evenings. When you aren't playing, you are free to kibitz at no charge, and what a learning experience that can be!

Whether you prefer rubber bridge or the challange of duplicate in groups of 40 to 4,000, the object is the same: to enjoy this wonderful game we all love— so let's all Play More Bridge!

Test Yourself

Your opponents are vulnerable. You are not. There have been two passes. What will you do with the following hands?

1. ♠ Q 10 9 8 7 4 3 You will open three spades
   ♥ 6   (you would even make this
   ♦ 9 4   bid in first or second posi-
   ♣ K J 2   tion). If in fourth position, of
                      course, you pass.

2. ♠ Q 10 9 8 7 4 3 In third position, you will
   ♥ 6   open one spade—*not* three
   ♦ K 4   spades.
   ♣ K J 2

3. ♠ K J 2   Bid three diamonds *only* in
  ♥ 6   third position. Pass any
  ♦ Q 10 9 8 7 4 3 other position.
  ♣ 9 4

4. Your opponents are vulnerable. You are not. The bidding is as follows:

OPPONENT	YOU	OPPONENT	PARTNER
1 spade	pass	2 spades	pass
?			

What will you do now?

  ♠ 7 3   You will bid two no trump—
  ♥ 2   the unusual no trump asking
  ♦ K Q 9 7 3   partner to bid his longer
  ♣ A J 6 5 2   minor suit.

5. Your opponents are vulnerable. You are not. The bidding is as follows:

OPPONENT	YOU	OPPONENT	PARTNER
1 spade	pass	1 no trump	pass
2 spades	?		

What will you do with this hand?

  ♠ VOID   You will bid two no trump—
  ♥ 7 6   (unusual) and partner will
  ♦ A 8 6 5 3 2   bid his longer minor. His
  ♣ K 10 7 6 4   length may well be in the
                   major suits, but he must bid
                   a minor.

14

SUMMARY OF LAWS OF CONTRACT BRIDGE

It would take up too much space in this book if we printed all the laws of contract bridge, so we will only include here the rules dealing with the most common things that come up at the bridge table through error or carelessness. We should know whether or not a penalty is involved in certain situations.

The ACBL publishes an official *Laws of Contract Bridge* which you may wish to have. The following is only a summary.

When do we have a redeal?
The deck is redealt:
1. Any time any card is exposed before the deal is completed.
2. If it is discovered before the deal is completed that the wrong deck was used or the wrong person is dealing.
3. If it is discovered before the *play* is completed that one player picked up too many cards, or one too few, or that the deck was imperfect. (If a player discovers during the play that he has only 12 cards, and the 13th is found on the floor or in the other deck, the deal stands.)

When may you change your bid?

When any player makes a slip of the tongue and changes in the *same breath,* like "one diamond—I mean one heart," it is OK and the bid may be changed.

When is a card considered played?

1. Any card that declarer touches in the dummy hand (except to arrange them) is considered played.
2. Any card that a defender holds in such a way that his partner can see the face is considered played.
3. Any time declarer holds a face card up touching (or near) the table, it is considered played.

When may we look at a trick?

After a trick has been taken and turned down, a player may see it *only* if neither he nor his partner has played to the next trick.

What may dummy do?

1. He may call attention to any irregularity, but only *after play* is complete.
2. He may try to *prevent* an irregularity (by cautioning declarer not to lead from the wrong hand, or asking about a failure to follow suit before the revoke becomes established).

NOTE: Dummy loses *all* privileges if he looks at his partner's hand or an opponent's hand.

What happens when you pass out of turn?

1. If you pass before anyone has made an opening bid, the only penalty is that you must pass at your first turn.
2. If you pass when it was another player's turn to call, and your pass is not accepted by your left hand

opponent, your pass is cancelled and the auction goes back to the proper player. If it was your right hand opponent, he bids what he chooses, and the only penalty is that you must pass this time. But if it was your partner's turn he may bid whatever he wishes, but you must pass for the rest of this hand and there are lead penalties.

What happens when you bid out of turn?
1. If no one else has either passed or bid and the player to your left was dealer, the auction reverts to the proper player, and when it's your turn you may do whatever you please; but partner must pass for the entire hand and there are lead penalties.
2. If you bid when it's your right hand opponent's turn, then, if he passes, you repeat your bid and there is no penalty. But if he bids, you may do whatever you please, but partner must pass at his next turn.
3. If you bid when it's your partner's turn, then partner must pass for the whole hand and you may do whatever you choose, but there may be lead penalties.

What happens when you make an insufficient bid?
If you make a bid that is not higher than the previous bid and your left hand opponent does not accept it, your bid is cancelled and you may do any of the following:
1. Make your bid barely sufficient in the same suit. (There is no penalty.)
2. Make your bid sufficient in any suit you wish or pass, but your partner must pass for the rest of the time and there may be lead penalties.
Of course, your opponents may accept your bids or passes out of turn, or insufficient bids if they wish, and if they do so there is no penalty.

211

What happens when a card is exposed at the table?
1.   Declarer may expose cards without penalty, provided they are not "played."
2.   When defender exposes a card, it becomes a "penalty card" and is placed face up on the table. It must be played at the first legal opportunity.

What happens when defender leads out of turn?
1.   The declarer may accept the lead and play from his own hand or dummy's, depending on whose turn it is.
2.   He can choose not to accept the lead, and the card improperly led is a "penalty card." Declarer may require or forbid the lead of that suit by the partner of the offender.

What happens when declarer leads out of turn?
1.   When declarer leads from the wrong hand, the lead may be accepted by defender (if he wishes) by playing a card on the lead or stating that he accepts the lead.
2.   Defender may call the lead from the correct hand and declarer must lead a card of the same suit (if possible) from the proper hand—but he is not required to play the card that was improperly led.

What happens when there is a revoke?
A failure to follow suit, when you could have, may be corrected any time *before* either the offender or his partner plays to the following trick. If this is done, there is no penalty, but the card mistakenly played (by defender) becomes a "penalty card." If declarer is the offender and makes the correction in time, there is no penalty. It is impossible for dummy to revoke. All players are responsible for seeing that dummy follows suit.

212

1. When a revoke has been established, it may not be corrected. If the offending side won the revoke trick, that trick, plus one of any subsequent tricks won are given to the non-offenders. If the offenders did not win the revoke trick, one of any subsequent tricks won is given to the non-offenders.

2. There is no revoke established on the twelfth trick.

3. There is no penalty for a second revoke in the same suit by the same player.

When a revoke costs the non-offenders more tricks than they are given by this law, the offending side should transfer additional tricks until equity is restored.

15
SCORING TABLE

Scores Above the Line

Overtricks

	Not vulnerable	Vulnerable
Undoubled	Ordinary trick value	Ordinary trick value
Doubled	100 per trick	200 per trick
Redoubled	200 per trick	400 per trick

Additional bonus

For making any doubled or redoubled contract   50

Honors

4 trump honors in any one hand	100
5 trump honors in any one hand	150
At no trump, 4 aces in one hand	150

Slam bonuses

	Not vulnerable	Vulnerable
Small slam	500	750
Grand slam	1000	1500

Penalties for undertricks

	Not vulnerable	*Vulnerable*
Undoubled	50 each trick	100 each trick
Doubled	100 first trick, 200 each additional trick	200 first trick, 300 each additional trick
Redoubled	Twice the doubled penalty	Twice the doubled penalty

Rubber bonus

When the rubber is won by two games   700
When the rubber is won by two games to one   500

Unfinished rubber

Bonus for a side with a game   300
Bonus for a part score in an unfinished game   50

Scores Below the Line

Spades or hearts	30 points for each trick over six
Diamonds or clubs	20 points for each trick over six
No trump	40 points for the first trick over six, 30 for each additional trick over six

If the contract has been doubled, multiply the trick score by 2; if redoubled, by 4.

16
GLOSSARY OF BRIDGE TERMS

ACBL—American Contract Bridge League. The organization which conducts tournaments and also records the master points received by players in the United States.

Above the line—scoring points that don't count toward game.

Artificial bid—a bid that asks for—or gives—specific information rather than suggesting the final contract.

Auction—the bidding process. It is ended when there are three consecutive passes.

Balance—reopening the bidding in the fourth position.

Balanced distribution—a hand that does not have a singleton or void, and not more than one five-card suit.

Below the line—scoring points that count toward game.

Bid—an agreement to win a certain number of tricks in a stated suit or at no trump, or the statement of that intent.

Blackwood—a convention used to ask for aces when investigating slam possibilities. It begins with a bid of four no trump.

Block—happens when you can't take tricks in a long suit because you won a trick in the wrong hand.

Board—a tray that holds the four bridge hands in pockets and is used for duplicate play.

Body cards—sevens, eights, and nines (they fatten up your hand).

Bonus—any premium other than the actual tricks scored.

Book—the first six tricks taken by declarer. For defenders, a book is one trick fewer than enough to set declarer's contract.

Business double—penalty double.

Call—any bid, double, redouble, or pass.

Come-on—a card that encourages partner to continue a suit.

Contract—final bid of the auction.

Control—a holding which prevents the opponents from cashing tricks in a suit. (An ace or void shows first round control; a king or singleton shows second round control.)

Convention—an agreement to give an unnatural meaning to a particular bid or play.

Cover—to play a card higher than the one already played.

Cross-ruff—trumping two suits, one in each of the partner's hands.

Cue bid—an artificial bid demanding game or showing a control.

Cut—the person to the right of the dealer separates the shuffled deck into two stacks and the dealer places the half that was originally on the bottom of the deck on top of the other half.

Deal—distribution of 13 cards to each player in a clockwise manner.

Dealer—the player who deals the cards.

Declarer—the player who wins the contract and plays the hand.

Defender—opponent of declarer.

Defensive bidding—bidding by opponents of the opening bidder.

218

Defensive tricks— cards expected to take tricks at any contract.

Discard—playing a card which is not in the suit led and is not a trump.

Distribution—the way cards are divided into suits.

Double—a call that increases the value of overtricks or undertricks at the opponent's suit bid.

Double finesse—a finesse against two missing high cards.

Double jump—a bid two levels higher than you need to make to overcall the preceding bid.

Double raise—a raise in partner's suit of one more than necessary.

Doubleton—two cards in a suit.

Down—failing to make the bid contracted.

Draw trumps—lead the trump suit until the opponents have none.

Duck—to deliberately lose a trick.

Dummy—declarer's partner.

Duplicate bridge—a form of bridge where all players play the identical hands, which move from table to table in duplicate boards.

Duplication—both partners have values in the same suit so they cannot be of use, such as a doubleton in both hands.

Echo—the play of a high card followed by a low card in the same suit.

End play—forcing the opponent to help you by giving him a trick, so that he must lead to you.

Entry—a high card or trump which permits a hand to gain the lead.

Escape suit—a second suit that may be bid if the first suit is doubled by the opponent.

Exposed card—a card played, or exposed, by mistake which then becomes a penalty card.

219

False card—play of an unusual card, made with the intention of deceiving the opponents.

Finesse—trying to win a trick when there is a higher card in one of the opponent's hands.

Fit—supporting cards in the same suit held by partner.

Follow suit—playing a card of the same suit as the card led.

Force—a bid which forces a bid from partner.

Forcing pass—a pass made by one partner when it is obvious from the bidding that the partnership holds most of the cards in that deal. This forces the other partner to decide whether to double the opponents or bid higher.

Fourth hand—(1) when bidding, the player on the dealer's right; (2) when playing, the last player to play on a trick.

Freak—a hand with wildly distributed cards.

Free bid—a bid made when partner would have another chance to bid even if you pass.

Free double—a double of a bid when the opponents have reached game.

Game—contract which scores 100 points below the line.

Gerber Convention—a bid of four clubs which requires partner to show the number of aces he has (used for no trump contracts).

Go down—fail to make the bid.

Grand slam—contract to take all 13 tricks.

Grand slam force—a bid of five no trump when *not* preceded by a four no trump bid and after the partnership has agreed on a trump suit.

Guarded honor—an honor with enough low cards in the suit so that it cannot be caught by a higher honor.

Hand—(1) the cards dealt to a player, or (2) any deal of the 52 cards.

220

High-low—the play of a high card followed by a lower one in the same suit (see echo).

Hold up—refusal to win a trick when you could do so.

Honor cards—any ace, king, queen, jack, or ten.

Honors—four trump honors in one hand (100 points above the line) or five honors in one hand (150 points above the land) and at no trump, all four aces in one hand (150 points above the line).

Informatory double—a double (better known as take-out double) that requests partner to bid.

Insufficient bid—a bid not high enough to outbid the opponents' previous bid.

Interior sequence—a sequence in the same suit with a higher card.

Invitational bid—a bid which is not forcing but strongly urges partner to bid again if possible.

Jacoby Transfer—any suit bid (except two clubs) over partner's no trump open, which asks opener to bid the next higher ranking suit.

Jump bid—bidding more than necessary.

Jump shift—jump bid in a new suit.

Kibitzer—a person who watches four people play bridge.

Lead—the first card played to a trick.

Lead directing double—a double which tells partner what suit to lead.

Lead directing play—the play of a card, usually in the case of an obvious switch, which suggests to partner your preference for a lead.

Leader—first person playing to a trick.

Light bid—a bid made with less than the normal values.

Limit bid—a bid which shows within exact limits the strength of your hand.

Major suits—spades or hearts.

Make—take the number of tricks contracted.

Master—a player with at least 20 master points.
Master points—awards given in ACBL tournaments.
Match point—the method of scoring duplicate.
Maximum—a hand having the best possible values for the bid made.
Minimum—a hand having the least possible values for the bid made.
Minor suits—diamonds or clubs.
Misfit—a hand where neither partner can support the other partner's suit.
Negative double—a double made after partner has opened the bidding and the opponent has overcalled. This promises values in the two unbid suits and asks opener to bid one of them if possible.
No trump—a contract where there is no trump suit.
Not vulnerable—describes a partnership which has not scored a game.
Opening bid—first bid of a hand.
Opening bidder—the first player to bid.
Opponent—player who is not your partner.
Optional double—a double, usually over a preemptive bid, when partner of doubler makes the decision of whether to pass and make it a penalty double or bid and treat it as a take-out double.
Overcall—a bid made by the side that did not open the bidding.
Overtake—to play a card higher than partner's card when he has already won the trick.
Overtrick—trick made by the declarer in excess of the number of tricks needed to make the contract.
Pair—two players who are partners.
Part score—score less than game below the line.
Pass—make no bid, double, or redouble.
Passed hand—a player who has passed.
Passed out—a deal thrown in because all four players passed.

Penalty—a restriction placed on a side for violation of laws.

Penalty card—a card illegally exposed by a defender, left face up in front of him to be played at the first legal opportunity.

Positive response—a bid in response to partner's bid which shows strength.

Preemptive bid—a high-level bid on a weak hand.

Preference—a bid choosing between two suits partner has bid.

Psychic bid—a bluff bid based on nonexistent values.

Raise—a bid in the same suit partner has bid.

Rebid—player's second chance to bid.

Redeal—the same dealer deals the cards again after a mistake is made in the deal.

Redouble—multiply by two the value of a trick score or penalty score when the opponent has doubled.

Rescue—to make another bid when partner's bid seems hopeless—usually after he has been doubled.

Respond—make a bid in answer to partner's bid.

Responder—partner of the opening bidder.

Reverse—when suits are bid in backward order, the first suit must be longer and the hand must be strong.

Revoke—failing to follow suit when a hand contains a card in the suit led.

Rubber—when one partnership wins two games.

Ruff—to trump.

Ruff-and-sluff—declarer cannot follow to the lead of a suit in either hand, allowing him to trump in one hand and discard in the other.

Rule of Eleven—a device which one uses to locate high cards in a suit, based on a lead of the fourth best card of a long suit, usually against a no trump contract.

Sacrifice—overbid intentionally, expecting to be set, in order to prevent the opponents from scoring (usually a game or slam).

Safety play—a play designed to avoid, or limit, losing tricks.

Second hand—(1) in bidding, the player on dealer's left; (2) in playing, the person who is second to play to a trick.

Set—to defeat a contract.

Set up—to establish winners by forcing opponents to take their high cards.

Sequence—three cards in rank order (queen, jack, ten or ten, nine, eight, for example).

Shift—lead a different suit from the one started by partnership.

Signal—the play of a card to convey a message.

Singleton—one card in a suit.

Sluff—to discard.

Small slam—to contract to take all but one trick.

S.O.S. redouble—a redouble by the bidder who has been doubled at a low level, telling his partner he is in serious trouble and asking partner to bid.

Squeeze—force the opponent to discard a vital card which will cause him to lose a trick.

Stayman Convention—a convention used by the partner of the opening no trump bidder.

Stopper—a card in the opponent's suit which will win a trick.

Take-out double—double made in order to request partner to bid.

Temporizing bid—a bid made by the partner of the opener which will give the bidder a second chance to speak and show additional strength.

Tenace—two cards not in sequence (ace-queen for example).

Third hand—(1) in bidding, dealer's partner; (2) in playing, leader's partner.

Touching honors—honor cards adjacent to each other.

Trick—four cards played, one from each hand.

Trump—suit named in the final contract.

Trump echo—playing high-low in the trump suit showing another trump.

Unbalanced hand—hand containing a very long or a very short suit.

Undertrick—a trick bid but not taken.

Unusual no trump—overcall in no trump, asking partner to bid (usually a minor suit).

Void—having no cards in a suit.

Vulnerable—describes a partnership which has scored one game toward the rubber.

Yarborough—a hand which contains no honor cards.

226